Poe'
trini†

FREDERICK WILHELMSEN
is a young professor of philosophy at the
University of Santa Clara, California. He
says that "outside of reading and talking,
I have only one great passion: sailing";
and about this book he says "I wrote it out
of a sense of gratitude for what Belloc has
done for me personally and for the Catholic Revival at large. I wanted to introduce
his thought to a new generation that does
not really read him." He is married and
has three children.

HILAIRE BELLOC:
No Alienated Man

HILAIRE BELLOC:
No Alienated Man

A Study in Christian Integration
By Frederick Wilhelmsen

Sheed and Ward · New York · 1953

TO JACK MADDUX

PREFACE

POET, SAILOR, Grizzlebeard—this trinity sums up, not only the man who is Hilaire Belloc, but the vision of integrated humanity concretized in his work. Bellocian humanism is Hilaire Belloc grasped in the essence of his spirit, seen at the center of his being. Only a detailed biography will reveal to this generation the full flavour, the magnificence, of this latter-day Villon.

Nonetheless it seemed to me that the perfections symbolized by the Poet, the Sailor, the Grizzlebeard are not the peculiarities of one man whose life has spanned almost two ages. They are perfections essential to the integral completion of Christian humanity. With this thesis in mind, I wrote this book: an attempt not only to introduce the contemporary reader to Belloc, but also an attempt to disengage, from the vast corpus of Bellociana, those themes that are of permanent value.

What follows is not a biography, nor is it a book of literary criticism. It is, if you like, a "metaphysics of the concrete" seen through the eyes of a man rooted in the things that are.

CONTENTS

Chapter One

NO ALIENATED MAN

The Four Men: Natural Humanism

THE ANCIENT Arabs spoke of a creature having life in two worlds: his body was rooted in the earth, but his soul swept out across the horizons to a world beyond. Let us call him by his name: Man. This balance which is Man is a tension rarely maintained in the course of human existence.

Let us call the one who situates his destiny in this world, and who habituates his gaze to the things this side of the horizon, Aristotelian Man. Let us call the one who despises the limits of the horizons, and who contemplates the world beyond, Platonic Man.

This first alienation of man from himself was healed in the ancient world by the Incarnation. Aristotelian Man, like St. Thomas the Doubter, could put his fingers in the side of his Creator; and Platonic Man, like the mystic John, found the Word, but it was the Word made Flesh. Revelation restored to man the unity that was himself. *Anima naturaliter Christiana.* This unity was achieved as a reality both personal and corporate for a period of time in that small segment of the globe known as Western Europe.

Human unity was gradually lost, and a new man came

into being. This man has his life neither in the rooted things of the world nor in a heaven beyond. Nor is he Christian Man, man reconciled to himself. This new man looks neither outward and above nor outward and round about him. He looks within, and attempts to find his salvation by a penetration and purgation of the hidden depths of his own personality. This is Modern Man, man twice alienated from himself, and he has not yet found his soul. *"Je est un autre,"* said Rimbaud. "I IS an Other." And yet the Other which he is, is shrouded in darkness; and it is in this crucifixion of himself that Modern Man has come to see, without knowing that he sees, the hidden irony of the Cross.

Rimbaud was to wreak his vengeance on this Other he could not find by denouncing poetry, and by turning to what consolations the sands of Africa and the keel of a slave ship could offer an alienated man. He was a forerunner of what has become the dominant motif of the Western soul as expressed in its literature: the Man of Guilt.

Guilt is the effect of estrangement; it follows on a renunciation, explicit or implicit, of some dimension of the human spirit which is essential to the integral perfection of man. This renunciation has nothing to do with asceticism, which is a discipline sanctified and defined by the Christian tradition, having as its goal the flowering of human existence. The ascetic is an artist who prunes away the irrelevant so that the end may be achieved. Alienation is altogether different. It is the renunciation of something without which the end cannot be. Hence, wherever you find this sense of guilt so preoccupying modern man, you find a rupturing of the human heart, a positive surrender of some value which is consubstantial with achieved, completed, personal perfection. Being cannot be mocked with impunity.

A whole body of literature has grown up within the last seventy-five years devoted to exploring and understanding the estrangement of contemporary civilized man. That this body of art, chiefly found in the novel, should deal with the expatriate seems extremely significant of the crisis facing man today. One need only recall the world of Henry James to find an apt symbol for the modern dilemma. This New Englander left his American home to find himself in a Europe that existed chiefly in his imagination. Some of his best work is an attempt at penetrating into the restlessness and homelessness of the Western soul. James is full of trans-Atlantic crossings.

His short story "Four Meetings" brings out the paradox of alienation. It concerns a young New England school teacher who yearns for the day when she can see the Europe of her dreams. She succeeds after years of work and saving, but is tricked, when her boat docks in the Port of Le Havre, into turning over her money to a young man who claims to be a distant cousin. She returns to New England by the next ship. James ends the story on a note of delicate savagery: the wife of the cousin, a bogus countess from the streets of Paris, comes to America to live with and off the young school teacher, now disillusioned, alienated, but desperately maintaining the situation out of a sense of decency, and out of the need to hang onto the frame of an illusion, rather than face the irony of the complete nothingness of her existence.

The irony is deepened in that this aging school mistress of Boston Puritan antecedents symbolizes James himself in his relationship to the older culture that he sought to know, and yet never penetrated to its depths. James remained an alienated man. All of this suggests the true story, so heavy with possibilities, that G. K. Chesterton recounted about James.[1] Chesterton had taken a summer house in

Rye, and James, "after exactly the correct interval," made a formal call, accompanied by his brother William. Everyone talked politely of one thing and another, mostly letters, until a roar went up from the garden; two bearded, unkempt tramps burst in on the delicately poised teacups, and sang out boldly for beer and bacon. It was the introduction of Henry James to Hilaire Belloc, and to the reality of that European tradition that ever remained a stranger to the New Englander. Chesterton suggests that the profound significance of this encounter eluded Mr. James, whose subtle mind seemed incapable of coping with anything beyond the shadow of a reality. Belloc bulked too big for him.

He continues to bulk too big for the generation that has carried the estrangement of James to its preordained and lonely end. Belloc incarnated a sanity and a vigour that reached back to Chaucerian England and the Paris of François Villon for roots. For this reason he has always irritated the advance guard of spiritual decay. He seems too confident of himself, too dogmatic. There is a healthy earthiness sustaining all his work that is too solid, too full of substance for the intellectual attuned only to broken men. Belloc has fed himself on reality, and he has tasted its bitterness and its salt. He has affirmed being. In so doing, Belloc has accepted whatever can genuinely nourish and sustain the fabric of human existence. He is not starved.

There is to be found in his work no trace of that sense of guilt in simply being a man that so defines the modern spirit. Belloc's Christian conscience is keenly aware of the limitations of human perfection, and his soul is soaked in a healthy conviction of the fact that sin has rendered us all more or less ugly in the sight of God. Belloc wrote once that "man, being man, has a worm in his heart." He penetrated into the reality of evil and his healthy realism

and high integrity prevented him from surrounding sin
with the glamour of a "mystique." Guilt, for Belloc, was
the result of a failure in human nature; it was not rooted,
as it is for the contemporary mind, in the very fabric of
human existence. It is because of this that Belloc parts
company with the contemporary mind, which is almost
ashamed to be. Every other emotion, every shade of feel-
ing and nuance of thought can be found within his vast
literary output: irony, humour, a deep pathos that never
degenerates into sentimentality, hate, piety, rigorous logic,
a profound gravity that at times only Christian hope rescues
from despair, tenderness, love; all these in abundance, but
guilt—guilt in the mere fact of existence—is nowhere to be
found, because Hilaire Belloc is, in every sense of the term,
an unalienated man.

If Belloc is almost completely incomprehensible to the
post-war intellectual (even the post-war Catholic intellectual), the lack of understanding can be traced to the
amazing personal integration of the man, and to the lack
of a comparable integration today on the part of those most
representative of the modern spirit. The ambiguity of
Belloc's position in English letters is rendered still more
pronounced in that he spans three well-marked and sharply
differentiated generations, while his work deploys itself
over an extraordinary number of apparently diverse fields
of interest. To some he is known as the founder of the
Distributist movement in English economic thought. To
others he is the intransigent enemy of parliamentary government and monied aristocracy. In the field of letters, he
remains the author of *The Path to Rome* and of a host of
delightful essays that reveal a man profoundly at home in
the hills and fields of South England and the Latin Continent. To most, the name Belloc probably conjures up a
Catholic Apologetic, for the first time not defensive, but

aggressive, militant, and confident in the superiority and
the justness of its cause.

In time, Belloc encompasses not merely three generations, but two ages. To a youth maturing into manhood
in the second half of the twentieth century, his name may
mean an era that never was. Born in the year of the fall
of the third Napoleon and the proclamation of the German
Empire in the Hall of Mirrors at Versailles, Belloc marched
in the dust of the caissons of the Third Republic when the
return of the white flag of Bourbon still hung like a threat
and a promise over the fields of France. His first book was
minted in the presses while Victoria was still Queen
of England. In him the Oxford Movement of Newman
yielded its finest harvest, and Edwardian London was filled
with the sound of his laughter, the vigour of his person, and
the early splendour of his prose. He belongs to an age
now dead.

The total significance of the man cannot be grasped by
isolating him within his time, nor by analyzing separately
his accomplishments in the dozen and more disciplines in
which he laboured. The specific Bellocian theses—his
espousal of both French Republicanism and the monarchical principle, his distributist economics, his defence of
the Western continuity with Rome, his doctrine on the
relationship between Catholicism and Europe, his contempt and his arrogance before all things demonstrative
of the modern temper—march forth and deploy themselves
controversially as commanded by an essential, integrated
position that can only be called classical in the larger sense
of the word. It is for this reason that the causes for which
Belloc fought so long and so eloquently can be understood
in all their grandeur, and can be evaluated objectively and
with full sympathetic precision only if his cardinal intuition is explored and fully grasped. Above all else, Belloc

is an unalienated man: a representative of a rarely achieved ideal, that of the integrated Christian humanist.

The integrated man achieves himself by making his own all those dimensions of human personality and perfection which when isolated one from another seem mutually incompatible. Integration is a steady struggle. It is not usually characterized by any sudden and dramatic affirmation or negation; it does not lend itself easily to artistic depiction. Integration grows from within, and if it flowers in grace and the supernatural order, it has its roots in the hidden depths of natural man. The classical humanist spirit, whether it be found in the pre-Christian or in the Christian world, always aims at placing before man an ideal that is neither angelic nor animal, but human, and which is therefore limited in the way man is limited. It is an ideal oriented in harmony with the reserves of reality at hand to human beings. For the humanist hopes to unite perfections in the concrete order of existence which, if left to themselves, would tend to conflict. The Christian humanist places his faith and hope in the Incarnation not only as a doctrine to be believed, but as a Divine vindication of the intrinsic goodness of man and of the world in which he lives. He restores all things to God, not by suppressing them, but by seeing in them the Creative Act which is the patent letter of nobility to whatsoever is, in any sense, being. A Christian humanist realizes that he cannot be a Christian man unless he is first man, and hence his supernatural life is grounded in a natural life which has been harmonized. Unfortunately Christian humanism has more often remained an academic ideal than a reality, and in a day in which human dignity is more and more suppressed in a society increasingly inhuman in its techniques and accomplishments, a man who actualized within himself this ideal to an astounding degree should grow in significance.

Belloc's centralized personality was not given him; it was achieved. His realization of his own destiny does not appear as an easy victory, but as something battled for. It is precisely in that battle that its grandeur lies.

The most articulate and symbolic statement of the natural humanism underlying his militant Catholicism is to be found in Belloc's *The Four Men,* a curious "Farrago" written rather early in his career. This book reveals the necessity of harmonizing the separate drives in man if man would be himself. It faces man with the paradox of natural humanism: its insufficiency in the face of death. Man, after a struggle, wins the battle against personal alienation only to face an alienation that strikes at deeper roots: an alienation of his very self, of his very being.

The Four Men is a book filled with an earth-sadness, and an almost pagan prescience of the passing of things. A favourite theme of Belloc's, the mood of the second of November, All Hallow's Eve, the Night of the Dead, runs like a somber motif through the entire work. The South English countryside, the land of Sussex, the author's own county, is permeated with an autumnal gloom; the hills and the valley of Arun, the surf booming quietly in the night, the sea air stiffening the drama of things, all this is threatened by a dissolution, not so imminent as to rob nature of its beauty, but present enough to render more lovely the things that pass.

"Myself" sits in the inn *George,* "drinking that port of theirs and staring at the fire,"[2] and moved by thoughts of youth and of the river Arun, he arouses himself and resolves to be off to see his home once again. He is joined by an old man (still vigorous against the march of the years) who lets himself be known as Grizzlebeard. The following day, October 30, 1902, the two men are met by a Sailor, a fellow in the full flood of life, a singer of songs and a profound realist; and the company is completed by a Poet, a man with visions and no money. The Four Men join in a pilgrimage to "the land they know."

They pass through the Sussex weald regaling one another with stories and songs, and they speak of the "Worst and the Best Thing in the World." That night they rest in a hut. The next day is given over to good bacon and to the singing of many songs, among which is the incomparable "Bishop of Old Auxerre." It is in this fashion that they arrive by easy stages at the house of Myself, where they rest until the following morning. The next night, the first of November, finds them at a little inn, and Grizzlebeard engages a philosopher, a "metaphysician," in heated conversation over the ultimate causes of things.

On the second of November, Myself awakes "from a dream," and Grizzlebeard tells him solemnly that it is the day of parting. The Four Men walk slowly and silently through the mists until they take "that lane northward which turns through Redlands and up to the hill of Elstead and its inn."[3] Then they break bread together for the last time in the communion of friendship, and the Three, led by Grizzlebeard, part company from Myself, who until the very end protests and urges yet another day of comradeship. Grizzlebeard replies:

"There is nothing at all that remains: nor any house; nor any castle, however strong; nor any love, however tender and sound; nor any comradeship among men, however hardy. Nothing remains but the things of which I will not speak, because we have spoken enough of them already during these four days. But I who am old will give you advice, which is this—to consider chiefly from now onward those permanent things which are, as it were, the shores of this age and the harbours of our glittering and pleasant but dangerous and wholly changeful sea."

When he said this (by which he meant Death), the other

two, looking sadly at me, stood silent also for about the time in which a man can say good-by with reverence. Then they all turned about and went rapidly and with a purpose up the village street.

I watched them, straining my sad eyes; but in a moment the mist received them and they had disappeared.[4]

Myself hurries on "into the loneliness of the high Downs that are my brothers and my repose."[5] Alone, somewhat shaken and bitter in his dereliction, he passes quickly over the burial mounds of the old kings of Sussex.

I . . . felt the full culmination of all the twenty tides of mutability which had thus run together to make a skerry of my soul. I saw and apprehended, as a man sees or touches a physical thing, that nothing of our sort remains, and that even before my county should cease to be itself I should have left it. I recognized that I was (and I confessed) in that attitude of the mind wherein men admit mortality; something had already passed from me—I mean that fresh and vigorous morning of the eyes wherein the beauty of this land had been reflected as a tiny mirror of burnished silver. Youth was gone out apart; it was loved and regretted and no longer possessed.

Then, as I walked through this wood more slowly, pushing before me great billows of dead leaves, as the bows of a ship push the dark waters before them, this side and that, when the wind blows full on the middle of the sail and the water answers loudly as the ship sails on, so I went till suddenly I remembered with the pang that catches men at the clang of bells what this time was in November; it was the Day of the Dead.[6]

Pushing on in this mood, dark with the mystery of death and the soul, Myself comes at last to the platform over Barl'ton, where to the east stretch the Downs and to the south lies the sea. Brooding over the communion of man and his fields, Myself thinks of the children on the plain below just coming into the world he must soon depart. Putting pencil to paper, he gropes toward poetic expression of the chaos within him, and as his emotions are incarnated in verse a song of hope emerges. The Dead do not die. They remain, if only to people the land of their birth as ghostly influences from beyond the grave. And on this note of doubtful affirmation, the book ends almost as mysteriously as it began.

What is one to make of this strangely moving work? Considered artistically, the book is almost a literary curiosity, not only when viewed in the context of the Bellocian corpus, but even when situated in the larger field of English letters. There is nothing quite like it in modern literature, and Belloc's farrago cannot be judged by standards appropriate to the novel or indeed to any other *genre* familiar to contemporary criticism. On one level *The Four Men* is clearly patterned after the medieval allegory. The personages depicted are archetypes. Grizzlebeard is symbolic of the wise man of the folk, full of ancient lore, singing dirges of the race and of the passing of youth. He is the custodian of the household gods, and philosophy is not unknown to him. He stands for order, historical continuity, and he views existence with a realism born of age and wisdom. Grizzlebeard is the tribal count, the feudal baron, the landed squire: he is Tradition incarnate. The Sailor represents man's communion with the physical universe: he is the eternal adventurer, the spirit of romance. Although attached to Sussex, his eyes are in love with sudden landfalls and distant hills. He is the wanderer in all men. The Poet, lean in body and ragged in appearance, is a man whose visions trip him up; he is not at home in this world, but he belongs to that company of Eternal Poets, the Seers of Western Tradition, that reach back to Plato.

These Three are archetypes of Man, as Las Vergnas has pointed out,[7] and Belloc succeeds in maintaining their physical separation *visually* by delineating sharply distinct physical types, indicating distinct spiritual or psychological types. And yet the whole movement of action throughout the four days clearly indicates that these three must become one. On one level they are distinct men. On a deeper level they are Myself, and Myself is clearly Hilaire Belloc.[8] *The Four Men* is thus more than a mere allegory; it presents itself to us as a complexity of meaning: the three men are companions necessary to the welfare and happiness of Myself; they are Archetypes of Man, particularly Western Man; they are dimensions of the personality of Myself.

The identification of the Three with the One is achieved by Belloc through the use of irony, a device he frequently employed in a peculiarly French manner. The man called the Sailor is clearly of that calling: "these eyes of his were veiled with the salt of the sea." But he is not simply a Sailor, as he would be in a mere allegory. He composes finer verse than does the Poet, a fellow he good-naturedly despises for his singular *lack of perception:* a dual use of irony, in that the Poet fails in that precise attribute in which he would be expected to excel. Grizzlebeard, the sage, when asked what is the Best Thing in the World, replies: sleep. His intellectuality and wisdom are countered by a naive naturalism. Although personifications on one level, the Four constantly contradict their surface symbolism. This gives them individuality, and it also furthers their identification with one another and with the personality of Myself.

This ironic ambivalence ministers to the key significance of *The Four Men* which Grizzlebeard reveals in his assertion that "Estrangement is the saddest thing in the world."[9]

Myself must be joined by the Three Men in his journey through Sussex, his passage through life, because these three are essential to the fullness of his own personality: to its integrity and completion. Belloc seems to be saying that there is a Poet, a Sailor, and a Grizzlebeard in each of us.

Let them be nourished. Without the lifting of the soul to the horizons, without at least a confused sense of man's belonging to a world which is not this one, without the visions of the Poet, a man is starved. Without the spirit of adventure, of youth, the awakening to the hills and the sea and to the love of woman and the spirit of song, without these things, without the Sailor, a man is over-subtle and refined beyond health. He inclines to decadence, to false mysticism, and to a pride that feeds on itself. The Sailor baptizes the idealist metaphysician with a pint of beer in "the name of the five senses." He carries religion with a smile. And a man without a Grizzlebeard is a man without home, without traditions, without accumulated wisdom. He is a man without a past, unmarked by distinction. He lacks roots and is alone.

Hilaire Belloc's initial integration is seen in this human trinity which is one. What heightens the significance of *The Four Men* is the almost total lack of a comparable integration on the part of that intelligentsia most representative of the modern Western world. Because of the religious rupturing of the Christian center of European society, even natural man lies broken in pieces, and the pieces continue to splinter with the passing of time. While this is not the place to probe exhaustively the causes of this fissioning of the human spirit, the fact might well be called the Great Evidence of the age.

The alienation of modern man has resulted on the natural level, because these three are not one. Myself is not Myself, but is an Other. Estranged from his past, uprooted from the land of his fathers, cut away from his origins, modern man is largely a stranger lost in a wilderness of pavements. He lacks a Grizzlebeard. He has not that bond of family of which T. S. Eliot speaks: "A bond which embraces . . . piety towards the dead, however obscure, and a solicitude for the unborn, however remote."[10] Abstracted from the actual existence of things by a science intent on constructing its own universe, he has been told that the Sailor in him, the man "of the five senses," is a naive realist who is duped by appearances that are not what they seem to be. Existence can be for him only Nothing, and this last alienation clothes Guilt with the dignity of a philosophical category. Existentialist man, modern man as mirrored by Sartre and Camus, is the final broken man. The alienation of the Poet is probably the most terrible of the lot: told that he must construct his own universe by a criticism and an aesthetics rotten with Idealism, he labours under the impossible burden of aping God, and ends frequently enough by playing the Devil. That is why a man must exorcise the Poet in himself and turn to a life of action as in Rimbaud, or to a life dedicated to the ideals of an outmoded Enlightenment as in Thomas Mann.

Mann's Tonio Kröger is told by Lisawetta Iwanowna that his guilt stems from the fact that as an artist he is alienated from conventional society. Adrian Leverkühn keeps his art only at the price of selling his soul to Satan. Conrad's Heyst, faced with self-betrayal to a philosophy of aloofment from existence, can do nothing but effect the final alienation: suicide. Sartre's heroes, all damned quarter-men, quiver viscously in closed places without exit. The modern intellectual seems driven to carve the human form into pieces, and then to worship in trembling the suffering he has himself caused.

Thus vigour has departed from art, and evil itself is given over to clinical weariness. Literary reputations are gained in proportion to one's "sin mystique," and one would think, contrary to the express words of Saint Paul, that conversion to Christ must follow on a season in hell. Suffering is the fashion, and a well-turned cross is one's ticket of admission to a literati that makes capital of the Crucifixion. It is the contemporary version of the thirty pieces of silver.

Yet those who have gone through this darkness and who have come out again into the world of being opening out to the Being of God, can understand the tragedy of the modern soul. It is a tragedy rooted in a profound misunderstanding of the nature of being and knowledge. Precisely where the tragedy begins is shrouded in mystery, but it may perhaps be said that Joseph Conrad stands at the crossroads where Western man deserted the last remaining traditional values and struck out into the unknown. Conrad's brilliant short story, "The Secret Sharer," is both symbolic and symptomatic of the crisis of alienation modern man invented for himself.

A young sea captain, new to his exalted position as master of a full-rigged ship, finds a man of his own years clinging to the bow of the vessel. Alone and still somewhat unsure of himself before his veteran crew, the captain's heart goes out to the swimmer; unknown to his crew, he hides the fellow aft in his cabin, only to discover that he is harbouring a fugitive. The man is guilty of the unpremeditated murder of one of the sailors who served under him in a nearby vessel in which he had been chief mate. The captain looks upon the escaped sailor as his double, and he feels in some strange way that he *is* this other, this criminal. In order to find himself, he must rid himself of his "double." He permits the fugitive to escape by swimming ashore, by means of a daring maneuver in which he almost destroys his ship by sailing her within striking distance of the land, before bringing her about on the new tack. When the vessel comes about on her new tack, just short of piling up, the captain sees that his strange friend and double has escaped by swimming to the land. A confidence in himself surges through him, and he knows that he is now Master indeed. Thus the captain discovers himself in the Other; but the Other had to be exorcized in order that the Captain, Man, could genuinely become himself.

Modern man, mirrored in the modern artist, realizes his destiny by casting out the other selves that he finds in his soul. By an extension, contemporary atheist existentialist philosophy teaches that *all* others—things, and persons—are set over against the self, threatening its existence: the world is a hedge of hard spikes aimed at the heart of the person, menacing it with otherness. All values, all wills, and all being together are but the positive nothingness of the Myself. They are one's non-being. The philosophy of Sartre (a symptom of a universal malaise), in which the "in itself" is discovered as the negation and the opposite of the "for itself," presents a world in which the very discovery of personality is constituted by an estrangement of man from existence. The alienation of the soul is the condition of its destiny. Only in nausea, anguish, disgust and dread can man learn that to be himself is not to be anything else. We are all Strangers, even to our own consciousness of ourselves.

If "The Secret Sharer" symbolizes, even obscurely, the birth of the New Man, *The Four Men* is the last picture of the Older Man—the Man of Christendom. Belloc's position takes on an added interest when it is seen to be the exact opposite, point for point, of man's situation in the world as conceived by contemporary literature and philosophy. Myself is rendered one and whole in becoming these Others, without which Myself cannot be Myself. In becoming the Poet,[11] Myself enters into a world of beauty and of all those visions that have ever stabbed at the heart of man calling him to a world only vaguely seen. In becoming the Sailor, Myself takes his stand within the physical universe of things: the universe of being. In becoming the Grizzlebeard, Myself conquers the past, and transcending the world of space, he enters into the dimension of time wherein he is one with his fathers and the ages.

Thus Belloc's *Four Men* might be called Thomistic; not in the sense that Belloc is a professional philosopher, but simply that his vision is oriented in the direction Aquinas' was, in the direction any Christian's is—toward reality. The revelation of the self to itself is had in knowing things other than the self. This is indeed the very definition of knowledge as it has been understood in the Western World: man knows himself in knowing other things, and to know is to be, or to come to be, the Other as Other. I first know what is not myself, and in the not-myself I am revealed to myself. I conquer the distance between myself and the Other by feeding on all things and values, for being is the proper nourishment of man. Unless I forget myself in the Other, I shall never be Myself. He who would gain his soul must lose it.

The Four Men represent the natural and classical foundation of Belloc's personal integration. He makes his own these archetypes of Western Men of that Western culture in which human nature most fully came into its own. The Poet, the Sailor, and the Man of Wisdom are the classical unities that underlie traditional Christian values. Belloc's Poet is as old as the Republic: he is less a man of art than a man of dreams; Belloc's Sailor looks to Homer; and Grizzlebeard, while English to the core, echoes the Augustan strains of Virgil.

Myself is one with himself in these companions. But all the comradery, the good fellowship, the hearty wisdom, and the love exchanged between friends is threatened by what one might call the possibility of classical or human alienation. Man is not his own enemy in Belloc's farrago;

Death is the enemy. The campfire blazes in the woods and the inn is full of decency and laughter, but the universe in the background breathes mutability and is marked for the harvest. The seasons rise and fall. Generation issues into corruption and the rich leaves of autumn prefigure the coming of death. Even the County of Sussex, marked for eventual dereliction, will yet outlive man.

Myself finds his soul in these companions, who part from him after Grizzlebeard warns Myself, Man, to meditate Death. Then "the mist received them and they had disappeared." Myself, troubled in spirit, faces the dilemma Everyman faces. Must this humanity, found and achieved in these four, be swallowed up in the mists? Must alienation, "the saddest thing in the world," claim the soul in the end? Why discover ourselves and then come to realize that we have found an illusion? We cannot come to be ourselves finally unless Death itself die in the end. The Night of the Dead has always been the night of their return, and Belloc implies throughout his closing chapter that this prefigures eventual immortality. He states this more explicitly in an essay from *Hills and the Sea* that is given over to meditating the meaning of autumn.

. . . at this peculiar time, this week (or moment) of the year, the desires which if they do not prove at least demand—perhaps remember—our destiny, come strongest. They are proper to the time of autumn, and all men feel them. The air is at once new and old. . . . The evenings hardly yet suggest (as they soon will) friends and security, and the fires of home. The thoughts awakened in us by their bands of light fading along the downs are thoughts which go with loneliness and prepare me for the isolation of the soul.

It is on this account that tradition has set, at the entering of autumn, for a watch at the gate of the season, the Archangel; and at its close the day and the night of All-Hallows on which the Dead return.[12]

It is only when life is lived close to the senses, and when the intelligence is brought to bear immediately on what is yielded to man through the body, that the paradox of sadness in created beauty can be brought home in all its delicacy and inexorableness. Page after page of Belloc's writing, from early youth to old age, is troubled by a deep melancholy, heightened by his profound communion with the things of his world: English inns, old oak—polished and sturdy, rich Burgundy, the sea and ships that sail, the smell of the tides. These loves run through Belloc's essays as recurrent themes, testifying to a vision, movingly poetic, that is classical in its simplicity. His gaze is rooted in the primal things that have always nourished the human spirit: in the things at hand.

Every pleasure I know comes from an intimate union between my body and my very human mind, which last receives, confirms, revives, and can summon up again what my body has experienced. Of pleasures, however, in which my senses have no part I know nothing.[13]

Here is a man who believes that great beauty is best found in the common: the common transfigured. This is the food which is the proper nourishment of man. Here peace is at hand. And yet this grasp of natural beauty in Belloc sharply points up the paradox with which the last chapter of *The Four Men* is concerned. The more sane man becomes in taking to himself those perfections needed for his fullness, the more bewildering appears his plight. His personal integration demands the final unalienation of immortal happiness; and yet happiness eternally possessed, man's only possible goal, is a hope and a conviction that attaches itself to the things which pass. Why, Belloc asks time and again, does the fatherland come home to us most poignantly when we are moved by the presence of mortality? Why should the symbol of the everlasting both

partake of the blessedness it promises and attest thereby
to its own temporal destiny?

A man goes into an ancient inn hidden in the hills of
South England. His soul receives a benediction and he is
at peace. He finds peace *there*, Belloc continually insists.
This is not the device of a litterateur. It is a reality which
carries along its own inexorable insufficiency. Man feeds
on being, and the being he feeds on fills him with longing.
He is nourished for a little while, only to hunger again.

"The Sign of the Lion," an essay rich in grave solemnity,
is given over to a consideration of this perennial dilemma.
The author, again "Myself," engages a stranger in conversation. The two sit before a great fire in the old common
room, and they consider a paradox: why does man try to
make the sign of eternal happiness bear the impossible dignity it signifies? These two have sought rest in this inn, and
from all sides the mortality of this mirror of immortal peace
floods in on them. They are filled with a somber realism.

Once more, in the essay "Harbour in the North," a
stranger appears before the author. Belloc has brought his
cutter under a long seawall, and he meets there another
small vessel. The pilot of this ship declares that he is off
to find a permanent refuge to the north in a harbour of
whose fame he has heard.

. . . Then he went on with eagerness, though still talking low:
"The voyage which I was born to make in the end, and to
which my desire has driven me, is towards a place in which
everything we have known is forgotten, except those things
which, as we know them, reminded us of an original joy. In
that place I shall discover again such full moments of content
as I have known, and I shall preserve them without failing."[14]

The seaman's stores were laid on board, and he was determined that "he should set sail before morning and reach
at last a complete repose." Belloc answers him from his

own boat—the Ship of Mortality: "You cannot make the harbour . . . It is not of this world."[15]

Man is unified in his own being. He is at one with the good things of this world—his habitation. But he is a creature of soul as well as body, and this world is at once a half promise of an eternal destiny and an image of human mortality. Such are the two *natural* elements of the Bellocian vision, and they define felicitously the best in classical humanism: an acceptance of human nature and of its home, and a realist understanding of the limits of finite perfection. Belloc is earth-rooted, and this renders him happy and melancholy by turns. It is the fate of every humanist, and it is not difficult to see why Belloc suggests Samuel Johnson. Johnson was not a mystic but a humanist, and he is therefore what seems to some a curious mixture of idealism and realism, virtue and cynicism, faith and skepticism. So too with Belloc.

Significantly enough, Johnson has been linked with both halves of the Chester-Belloc. Johnson and Chesterton are linked together through their striking Englishness; abstracted, careless in dress, gigantic, they both call to mind the London of Fleet Street. But for all his associations with London, Belloc remains either the man of Paris or the man of the hills of South England. His love of nature and his affinities with life lived close to the soil and the sea provide the key to understanding the differences between the Bellocian and the Chestertonian vision. The two comrades fought together for years for the same truths, but it would be naive to assume that they both saw these truths in the same way. Chesterton was pre-eminently a speculative thinker, but he invested his thoughts with all the warmth and cockney glamour of the gas-lit and fog-filled London he loved. He went through life more abstracted from things than engaged with them, and he took whatever was at hand without reflection: if he drank great quantities of wine, he also drank deeply of water, if water were put before him. But when Chesterton shook himself out of his reveries and gazed on reality, then miracles happened. Romance is always something brought to a thing, and Chesterton invested the whole world with the great goodness of his heart. Chesterton in contact with a *thing*, be it a lamppost or an umbrella, was like the fuse that ignites a Roman candle. Anything at all set his intelligence off on a brilliant fireworks of paradoxes that penetrated into the heart of reality. He was a symbolist, and the inner meaning of creatures was never hidden from his concentration. This world diaphanously let through the glories of another order, and Chesterton could see God in a gable. If his world looks like a pasteboard toy theatre created by a father for the sheer joy of his children, Chesterton could demonstrate that the analogy was strictly true. If the toy was out of order and deranged, the contrast fingered more sharply than ever the primeval origin of the world in goodness.

Chesterton's vision was metaphysical, as Mr. Hugh Kenner has suggested;[16] broadly speaking, it was mystical as well. The same cannot be said of Belloc. His vision is more poetic than metaphysical. On one level almost a rationalist, on another level—the level that finds him communicating with the world in which he exists—he is profoundly tender and awed before the loveliness of creation. It is the mark of a philosopher that he can see significance apart from the symbol, whereas it is characteristic of the poet to cling fast to the concrete structure of his intuition. Belloc is too much in love with things to use them as stepping-stones to eternity. He sees eternity in their very passing, and this is the root of the much-misunderstood Bellocian irony. Throughout most of his better essays and in his masterpieces such as *The Path to Rome* and *Hills and the Sea* one can sense an awesomeness and love of finite beauty that reveals itself in a style chaste and unadorned in its expression of tenderness and reverence before the things which are. Belloc drank at the sources of great rivers. He worshipped the tides.

Belloc saw things, but Chesterton saw through them. This is not to say that one is greater than the other, but it is to declare their fundamental difference.

Belloc's close union with the passing universe heightens the great classical humanist dilemma that underlies all his thought: man is threatened by death. Like everything genuinely classical, this is a universally human paradox. The more fully does man achieve his earthly destiny and bring to a certain pitch of perfection and actuality the possibilities originally latent within him, the more fully is he aware of the irony of temporal existence. From this follows the perennial preoccupation with the passing of beauty and the inevitability of death. Genuinely Roman, the vigour and the iron ring of the Bellocian affirmations are tempered in a lyricism before the *lacrimae rerum*, and are frequently mellowed in somber meditation on the great fact of death.

In his biographies, Belloc brings to the famous death scenes of history a heightened sensibility born of that prolonged consideration. Read of the execution of Danton written in the fires of early youth; of the murder of King Charles I of England; of the conversion of the second Charles on the point of death. Read in *Elizabethan Commentary*, one of his final books, that passage in which he attempts to guess at the heart of his subject, and, in so doing, reveals himself: "She felt that she was ceasing to be herself and that is what probably most of us will feel when the moment comes to reply to the summons of Azrael."[17]

A brooding sense of inevitable personal death, prefigured by the passing of friends and the advance of age, haunts a great deal of his writing, and invests it with a solemn majesty that recalls again the great Doctor Johnson, a humanist who faced the end with bleak courage and somber faith. There is an essay in Belloc's *Towns of Destiny* titled "Cornetto, of the Tarquins" in which his emotional skepticism emerges into light in an almost pure state. Speaking of those tombs which are of the origins of us all, Belloc makes us aware of the "subterranean vision of death, the dusk of religion, which they imposed on Rome and from which we all inherit."[18] Humanism, even Christian humanism, must pay a price for its achievement of the earthly home, and that price, frequently enough, is the temptation to skepticism. "Then I thought to myself, as I looked westward from the wall, how man might say of the life of all our race as of the life of one, that we know not whence it came, nor whither it goes."[19]

The bourgeois world has romanticized death so that it can escape facing that most monstrous of indignities. Belloc, on the contrary, views death steadily as the threat to his humanity which must be explained without being explained away. The final destruction of that precious crucible of human existence, the individual personality, cannot be thought without contradiction. Everything in man is a drive toward being. If he is sane, man aims at becoming more and more himself, and to break the human fabric is to betray humanity itself. The Dead do not die, cries the old Roman in Belloc. But what can testify to this inner conviction when the senses themselves seem to mock the exigency of human nature for survival? Man ought to continue to be, but all man can see is the passing of things in the eternal rhythm of generation and corruption.

There can be no doubt that Hilaire Belloc was temperamentally a skeptic, at least throughout a good part of his career. It is a skepticism which follows on his classical

humanism. To be integrated in earthly existence is to conceive both the possibility of an eternal destiny and the
threat of the opposite. To be at home in this world is to
recognize the composite nature of man. The human soul
is not a Platonic idea, but the act of a body rendered human
by its union with the soul. To be fully aware of this, and
only the man who attends to the reality of the earthly part
of himself is so aware, is to experience a *sense* of annihila-
tion before the inevitability of death. This is not philosophy, but it is an attitude which is unmistakably human.
If to be myself is to be fully a man, then when I cease to
be a man at the moment of death, I shall cease to be myself. Aristotle never got clear of this problem, which can
be called the threat of classical alienation: the final alienation of man should he cease to be. "Death . . . shakes
and rends all that is human in us, creating a monstrous
separation and threatening the soul with isolation which
destroys."[20]

Final classical alienation, let it be insisted once again,
becomes a more pointed sword the more fully is human
integration achieved. Since alienation is never affirmed, but
is emotionally grasped as a possibility along with the hope
for personal immortality, classical man feels no sense of
guilt simply in being himself. If he is alienated in the end,
it will be too late for guilt. Temporal classical guilt results
from man's ceasing to be what he can be, and this defines
the nature of tragedy. Modern alienation, on the contrary,
is an alienation existing within a man who can be himself
only on condition that he is alienated. Hence he is aware
of guilt as the quasi-specific difference defining his existence. He is almost ashamed to be.

Classical humanism is basically insufficient, since man
cannot achieve, of himself, the fullness of his dignity.
Threatened from without by death, the humanist's integ-

rity is attacked from within by the wounds of sin that divide him from himself. Belloc never romanticized man, and he is so conscious of the *fact* of sin that his historical judgments frequently seem cynical. In a short story called "The Opportunity," he writes of three men that "each of these . . . being a man, had a worm at his heart, eating it out."[21] Courage excepted, the classical European humanist has no natural weapons with which to answer the final questions.

The humanist cannot escape into the mystical nihilism that has so fascinated the Eastern World, because his initial choice has been an election for all human values. Romantic irrationality, be it aesthetic, political, or naturalistic, is an insult to his reason. His world outlook is grounded in the being of the world accepted in its fullness, and in the achievement of his own being through his affirmation of the world in which he exists. He cannot, without betraying the light which has been given him, join the oriental drive to the beyond. He has too much respect for *who* he is, and for *where* he is. Only faith, a Faith that confirms and sanctifies the foundations he has built, and a Faith that fills with reality his hunger for an eternal destiny, can guarantee his fundamental vision: personal perfection and the happiness that issues therefrom. The classical humanist, the old European, sees the gigantic hoax contained in all the pantheisms and nihilisms that have come riding out of the deserts to assault the citadel he has built. They offer everything to man, provided he destroy himself in the darkness of a mysticism or a philosophy that is at bottom hollow with atheism and nothingness. The only immortality worth having is one that is personal and that unites man with a Personal God who can bestow happiness on the creature of His Image. Man is, and only He Who Is can slake his thirst.

The Path to Rome: Christian Integration

The Catholic Faith came to Hilaire Belloc from his birth to answer this humanist dilemma. Yet Faith came to him hard, and precisely because it did his final Christian affirmation has about it the resounding ring of iron: the iron which is the adherence of the will to a God unseen. If Belloc ever had what are called "religious experiences," or supernatural "consolations" to aid him on his pilgrimage, he has kept them sedulously to himself. He seems to appear, the more closely he is read, as almost an archetype of skepticism conquered.

There is a passage in *The Path to Rome* that would lead one to think this born Catholic went through a severe siege of skepticism during the confused time of youth. Years later, in at least two published works, he hinted at something approaching a reconversion in which he awoke to a more fully articulated understanding of Catholicism.

In the first place I was baptized into the Faith upon my birth, and have known it all my life. . . . Next, I have, though baptized into it and familiar with it from my earliest years, in some sense also discovered the Faith—but this I will not pursue as it is somewhat intimate, and hardly to the point; unless, indeed, it be to the point to tell those who read me and who are balancing, that I also have balanced.[22]

The same sentiment, once again guarded in reticence, is made in an essay written on the death of Chesterton.

I was not when I first met him as alive to the strength of that word "Catholic" as I am today; I myself have gone through a pilgrimage of approach, to an understanding in the matter. . . . Having said so much . . . I will leave it, for it is too personal and has been too prolonged.[23]

To a generation accustomed to the depiction of the psychology of grace, the personal reserve of the man, prolonged through a life devoted to religious controversy, is bound to be curious if not somewhat irritating. He reveals almost everything but the inner spiritual crisis. He apparently felt it was no one's business but his own. Nothing could be more typically Bellocian.

The Catholic Church appears in Belloc's thought, as given us in his writing, as the custodian of the Faith—of a Faith beyond himself, objective, out there, demanding acceptance because it is the Truth. Emotional skepticism is disciplined by a reason that must affirm that which is. Christ came, claimed to be Divine, died, and came back in three days from the dead. Such is the evidence, and it is ultimately traceable, through tradition and written testimony, to the Apostles who saw it with their own eyes. Faith is not established, as such, by personal experience nor by private speculations, but on an evidence which is a heritage common to all mankind. Emotion may aid or may block faith, but the act of faith itself is eminently reasonable, and it is the business of the will to rectify reason and not permit it to be swamped in the vagaries of subjectivism. Belloc's approach is by no means the only approach to religion, but it is one that is cold, hard, rational; the insight of a man with an intellect which is French in its incisiveness, directness, and confidence in itself. Such a faith is unbolstered by any natural religiosity, but for that very reason it presents a hard, diamond-like character, unyielding and dogmatic in its affirmations: a faith foreign to fashions, be they literary or philosophical.

In a letter written to Chesterton upon the occasion of the latter's entrance into the Church, Belloc compares the man of Faith to a man who walks through the rain at night, and who feels in his bones that he has gone thirty miles, but who knows well enough from his map and his reason that he has not travelled eleven.

I am by all my nature of mind skeptical. . . . And as to the doubt of the soul I discover it to be false: a mood, not a conclusion. My conclusion—and that of all men who have ever once *seen* it—is the Faith: Corporate, organized, a personality, teaching. A thing, not a theory. It.

To you, who have the blessing of profound religious emotion, this statement may seem too desiccate. . . . It is my misfortune. In youth I had it: even till lately. Grief has drawn the juices from it. I am alone, and unfed, the more do I affirm the Sanctity, the Unity, the Infallibility of the Catholic Church. By my very isolation do I the more affirm it.[24]

The early death of his wife whom he worshipped, the death of a son in World War I and then again of a son in World War II, the ever present and never fully overcome threat of personal poverty, the passing of the friends of youth, the dire fulfillment of his political and economic warnings which went unheeded, the apparent dryness of his religious life—all these tragedies struck his heart and isolated him from family, friends, political life, society, from joy. He never speaks of these things in his public writings, but they add to his integrated Catholic personality the steel of great character. He maintained himself in a desert.

From the very outset of his career, the Catholic center of Belloc's life appears as the spiritual hub from whence proceed the amazingly diverse spokes of his personality. The Faith is never glimpsed as a hope in the distance that calls him out of the secularist age in which he lived. The Faith is always present, informing and energizing his being, disciplining his irony, conquering his skepticism, and giving direction to his destiny. Nevertheless, a close reading of the Bellocian corpus reveals a shift in religious emphasis as the man advanced in years. In the earlier books, the humanizing role of Catholicism is the dominant motif: the Church is that corporate organism, Divine in origin, that alone accounts for the high culture of the older European civilization. She is the custodian of personal dignity, the ancient mistress that alone of all societies can harbour the human spirit and nourish it into its fullness. Through her, God offers temporal dignity and eternal salvation to man. But as Belloc grew older he sounded a new religious emphasis as he plunged more deeply into directly apologetic and controversial battle. Although the reality of Christian humanism is never forgotten, the Church emerges in his writing not only as the Divine instrument of human salvation, but more and more as the Truth of God, to which everything personal must be sacrificed, should events dictate such a course.

Belloc saw with unerring accuracy that the bulk of what he called "official history" in the English-speaking world was anti-Catholic. He attacked the thing bitterly, brilliantly, and at great cost to his reputation. He saw that the individualist, industrial, capitalist society of England was anti-human to the core. He attacked it. He grasped the anti-Christian meaning of Prussia, and he fought against this spirit from the North of Germany with intense vigour. He analyzed the anti-intellectual and therefore anti-Catholic bias that moved the "Modern Mind" in the bewildering complexity of that mind's activities. He detested the *Zeitgeist* which had surrendered the best man had: his power to reason, judge, and affirm; therefore it had lost the one sure road it had of discovering the Truth of God. Belloc became committed—the French artilleryman in the service of the Church. His intransigence rendered him a marked man. Shaw wondered why Belloc should waste his profuse talents in the service of the Bishop of Rome.

Wells noted critically his "partisan fanaticism." Some Catholic academicians, to gain for themselves the reputation of impartial scholarship and save their standing in the world of learning, disavowed him.

There is no doubt that Belloc entered into battle with his eyes open. If he was anything at all, he was a realist: he understood men and the motives that move them; he was aware of the doors opening to political and literary preferment. His brilliance was such that he could have risen to a Cabinet post through the Liberal Party. He could have carved out for himself an exclusively literary reputation, possibly as great as Conrad's. He could have become the recognized first historian in the Empire. He sacrificed it all and placed his sword at the service of the Church. It has been suggested that the decisive turning point in his career occurred when he delivered a fighting speech before Archbishop Bearne against the Liberal Government's intention to prohibit a Eucharistic procession through the streets of London.[25] At that time Belloc was a Liberal Member of Parliament, and the Tories thought that he would turn to them after his break with his own party. His political principles would not permit such a sellout. He went up to the platform a public figure, and came down an Apostle. "I begin to think this intimate religion as tragic as a great love . . . as tragic as first love, and (it) drags us out into the void away from our dear homes."[26]

Belloc's career as an apologist exemplifies the first paradox inherent in Christian humanism. Only the Incarnation can make man whole, but as the Incarnation issues into Calvary, so too must the whole man sacrifice himself to the service of the God-Man. The ascent of man to God is impossible without the prior descent of God to man, and the two meet at the Cross. Once this truth is lived, then the second paradox of Christian humanism can follow. The man who has given himself is paid back with his own gift: himself transfigured in the Divine Fires.

Belloc became himself in controversy. He warmed to the battle entered into freely, and his personality expanded before the prospect of facing all official England arraigned against him. It was a time in which things Catholic were neither popular with the masses nor fashionable with the elite. His opposition was enormous. Possibly he could have gained some concessions to his cause had he compromised; but Belloc never stooped to conquer. It is small wonder that Douglas Jerrold called him one of the last men in England who was, in the full sense of the term, not vulgar.

He became most widely known as a brilliant and somewhat brutal defender of the Catholic Order. But what is not so widely known is the fact that Belloc's vocation was erected on a delicate structure of human values accepted in their fullness, disciplined by an understanding of their limits, and welded into one by Faith. Belloc is not simply a Michael defending his beloved Church. His partisan belligerence masks his humanist complexity: he is really many men—a pagan Roman classicist—an English naturalist, a French rationalist, a soldier—a Catholic—one man.

The contrast between pagan humanism—man achieved on earth, but threatened by death—and Christian humanism —man achieved forever—can best be grasped by contrasting *The Four Men* with the great *Path to Rome*. In the former book, Myself finds himself in his companions, but having found himself he faces the threat of final isolation, the alienation of death. The somber beauty of the Sussex wood, the lonely Downs and the pounding of the tides, the time of autumn, symbolize the threat to the human person who is just coming into his own. Death is all around him, and Sussex itself is marked with the inexorable mutability attaching to a passing world. Although all Four Men are Catholics, their religion functions in the foreground, around the campfire as it were, as hardly more than a mythology. Immortality is hoped for, but is not affirmed clearly as a reality. Belloc achieved a brilliant artistic success in painting the dilemma of the ancient pagan, and the dilemma of every man, in a framework which is, on the surface, both Catholic and contemporary. He was able to do this because he remained throughout his life, on one level of his personality, the threatened Myself.

The Path to Rome, on the contrary, is most particularly the book of a Catholic man at home in Christendom. Man is in no sense alienated. Myself (here openly the author) is a member of the Church Militant, destined for the Church Triumphant. Belloc tramps through the Alps, down into the broad Italian plains, and his heart expands under the graciousness of Catholic skies. An abounding good humour flows into every event, conferring on the most trivial encounter the character of high adventure. Here is the picture of a man who has fought the battle for Faith, and who has been granted some share of peace. He still ponders the nature of the soul. A man so at home with mountains, good wine, and the laughter of friends will never approach the supernatural with the confidence of a contemplative. Belloc's delight is with the old Europe he loves so deeply, and if there be ecstasies beyond what he can see, he will "take them upon trust and see whether they could make the matter clearer in Rome."[27] The irony of this essentially somber spirit is relieved by a humour that is thoroughly Catholic in its simplicity.

This best of all travel books is vintage Belloc because it displays him in all the rich diverseness of his centralized personality. His grave mood, his Grizzlebeard, is constantly balanced by his robust vitality, by the Rabelaisian flavour of this latter-day Villon. He relishes existence with a zest that does due honour to the gifts of God; he laughs; he pontificates with mock solemnity; he trifles brilliantly with words (see the business about "windows"); he holds forth on the nature of Fools; and then he breaks into some of the loveliest lyrical prose in all English letters. And through all this adventuring and tramping runs a sanity that is almost more than human. If great beauty be the "common transfigured," as Belloc holds it to be, then this record of a shanksmare hike to Rome shall ever stand as a symbol of what man can be if he will only cease being other than himself.

The universe as seen by Hilaire Belloc in *The Path to Rome, Hills and the Sea,* and *The Cruise of the Nona* is a thoroughly Catholic universe: physical nature is grasped as good in its very being, and to this inner worthiness of all things there has been added the sacramental seal of the power of God. One can almost see the Papal blessing *Urbi et Orbi,* hanging like a benediction over the vineyards and hills of Italy as they embrace the man coming down from the cold heights of the Alps.

One can describe the Bellocian world no better than by saying that it is the total opposite of the world of Brunner, Barth, Kafka, and Kierkegaard. If Belloc's way of looking at things seems so strangely foreign when compared with the outlook of the contemporary intelligentsia, it is because the former is Catholic and the latter is lapsed-Catholic. The philosophy of the modern European is, as Edith Stein once said, "the philosophy of a lapsed-Catholic with a bad conscience." If Belloc sees the supernatural order as completely penetrating the natural order, it is because grace is seen as not destroying a nature essentially corrupted in sin, but as operating within man and flowering in his very gestures.

Dozens of times throughout his essays, Belloc's Catholic insight comes home to the reader, not as something super-imposed nor as something articulated conceptually, but as the very intelligibility of the man's work. He saw reality as a gift to be greeted and revered. There is nothing of the contemporary irritation with existence in Belloc. He is never shocked by being. He does not stumble guiltily through a world of spikes, hedged in by the sharp outline of nothingness. Human hypocrisy, greed, social injustice, the loss of economic and personal freedom, the pride of the rich: these sins arouse his ire and bring forth the great thunder of his hammer-like denunciations. But being has not sinned. It is the innocent one recalling all of us to the morning of the race, and to the promise of paradise re-gained. "If someone find a beautiful thing, whether done by God or by man, he will remember and love it. This is what children do, and to get the heart of a child is the end surely of any act of religion."[28]

If we would seek one symbol that best crystallizes the Bellocian affirmation, we would find it in wine. Belloc, tramping over the lands of Barbary, brooded long on the lost vineyards as he saw nothing but the vacancy of the desert. He turned and went back to that Europe he so loved, and he drank wine to her in his heart.[29] Wine called forth for him the Sacrament of the Altar and that one mo-ment in time when a passing world full of passing men was lifted out of the darkness. The mystical figure of wine seemed to him to sum up the Catholic affirmations, even to the heart of the Mysteries of the Faith.

The Bellocian vision, while poetic and religious, finds its completion in history. Belloc's grasp of the European past was something amazing, and it grew out of the need his personality felt for total integration. Man would remain starved if he did not make his past his own. In Belloc the ages became one. As the Church is something visible, exist-ing in space, and enduring in time, so also is the world that she has created something physical to be seen and handled like a Thing: something that perpetuates itself against mor-tality through a tradition that stretches back into the mists of antiquity.

A man's understanding of himself depends on where he steps into history; not mere academic nor *written* and cata-logued information, but the past as assimilated into a per-sonality, and as taking on the very existence of a man. When Belloc writes history he is one with the march of the West. Whatever was divisive of the unity of Christen-dom, even if dead and long conquered, receives at his hands a hatred that is almost personal. Belloc the soldier haunted the battlefields of the First Crusade, marked with his fingers the high point of the Mohammedan wave, and went with Napoleon into the Russian winter. He said once of a friend that "history had overlapped on him." He was describing himself.

All this does not make for dispassionate scholarship, but it makes for something vastly more important: it situates a man squarely in the path of history, and it renders him con-scious of all that has gone before to make him what he is. He becomes himself twice over. What contemporary writer speaks of the time when "we broke the back of Islam at Tours"?

Spiritual insight into the destiny of Christendom, added to an imagination that could vividly resurrect the past, were tools that rendered Belloc uniquely capable of pre-senting the drama of Europe to an age that largely had ceased living by the old Faith. But above their value in furthering his Christian vocation, they added to his theo-centric humanism further integration. The person who is unified in himself and in society through Faith is further enriched if he *is*, in a sense, all that has gone before. It was Belloc's good fortune that there was enough of the older Christendom physically in being for him to see at first hand. His historical perspective is uniquely realistic. He frequently deplored historical investigation that proceeded exclusively through written testimony. Such history is lacking in two things: the past is not brought back to us with sufficient vigour and colour, and the past loses its personal, human, integrative value, because history must be seen in *things* which now exist because of that which has existed.

History, therefore, once a man has begun to know it, becomes a necessary food for the mind, without which it cannot sustain its new dimension . . . But history, if it is to be kept just and true . . . must be continually corrected and moderated by the seeing and handling of *things*.[30]

Belloc's intensive preoccupation with Christendom is an interest not in a concept, nor in an abstracted framework nor an academic "problematic"; it is an engagement in an historical reality, to be *seen* and understood on the spot. Occasionally, as he stands in some place hallowed by past significance, he seems almost burdened by the grandeur of the task. See how he writes of the fascination of pursuing the Roman Road between Winchester and Canterbury:

For my part I desired to step exactly in the footprints of such ancestors. I believed that, as I followed their hesitations at the river-crossings, as I climbed where they had climbed to a shrine whence they also had seen a wide plain, as I suffered the fatigue they suffered, and laboriously chose, as they had chosen, the proper soils for going, something of their much keener life would wake again in the blood I drew from them, and that in a sort I should forget the vileness of my own time, and renew for some few days the better freedom of that vigorous morning when men were already erect, articulate, and worshipping God, but not yet broken by complexity and the long accumulation of evil.[31]

What he is proposing here and what he urges constantly is an historical recovery of the self, so that spiritual isolation will not claim the soul.

If modern man is isolated, and who can doubt that he is, his isolation stems from a variety of causes, some of which have been briefly indicated. Among others is the almost total loss of not only the reality of tradition, but of the sense of tradition, in industrial man. By industrial man, of course, one indicates not simply the man engaged in factory production. By industrial man one means that mechanical personality who has been fashioned by the age—a wound that few if any of us have escaped.

Without a steady tradition enduring through the passage of generations a man lives insecurely in a present which constantly ceases to be. The drive of his being towards an eternal destiny necessitates his finding an analogue of eternity. Without this, man is without moorings; he drifts and is alone; he is obscurely guilty of lacking something demanded by his nature. Without tradition, he is a victim offered daily to the cruelties of the moment.

Man has a body as well as a soul, and the whole of man, soul and body, is nourished sanely by a multiplicity of observed traditional things . . . Not only death . . . but that accompaniment of mortality which is a perpetual series of lesser deaths and is called change, is challenged, chained, and put in its place by unaltered and successive acts of seasonable regard for loss and dereliction and mutability . . . the perils of sickness in the body and even in the mind, anxiety, honour harassed, all the bitterness of living—become part of a large business which may lead to Beatitude. For they are all connected in the memory with holy day after holy day, year by year, binding the generations together; carrying on even in this world, as it were, the life of the dead and giving corporate substance, permanence and stability, without the symbol of which (at least) the vast increasing burden of life might at last conquer us and be no longer borne.[32]

Man's past has never been better known than it is today. Yet this knowledge is almost exclusively academic. It is encased in the great libraries of the civilized world, and it exists divisively in the minds of countless scholars. But it is no longer known *as a whole* that translates itself into the life of the community. In ceasing to be a tradition, the great story of the West has died; for the only existence the past can possibly have in a culture is traditional. A tradition is measured in a society by that society's consciousness of its own *symbols*, which render the tradition present to men. Contemporary industrial society has burgeoned within what was once Christendom, but having lost the old Faith, it has lost the old symbols, which now hang on precariously as *myths* and forms emptied of content. Industrial man has no tradition of his own to incarnate in song and stone, in the gestures of daily living. He has nothing to recall. As a result contemporary man is ruled largely by wayward myths that appeal to his subconscious drives. Political slogans, ideals gleaned from mass entertainment and ephemeral advertising dominate his urges, and create his conscious desires. Cinema heroes and contest winners give him an ever shifting hagiography in which nothing is so dead as yesterday's idol or this morning's news. Even the library that houses last week's paper is called "the morgue."

A society without a self-conscious tradition takes to worshipping the future. It adores that which has not been, and that which never is. If Shaw was a satirical mirror of the late nineteenth and early twentieth century, his friend Wells was its prophet. It is through Wells that the man of the twenty-fifth century came into his own. And Wells' most articulate critic in those days, throughout the whole of England, was Hilaire Belloc. Today Belloc's long battle against this drive away from our origins, his long fight to make the West conscious and proud of its past, has been partially vindicated, ironically enough, in our own generation. After World War II, with the threat of the atomic age, the prophets of the future have turned into prophets of doom. When thinking man looks ahead he does not see the age of superman, but the grim world of Big Brother and the phantasies of George Orwell. The future, if the present be not altered by a radical reaction, can only effect a "Servile State" which would be even more inhuman and barbarous than the coming society envisaged by Belloc when he first penned that now famous term in 1908.

Belloc had no doubts about the great Western Catholic tradition. He was absolutely convinced of its superiority—a superiority that extended to the economic and political orders as well as to the theological. Belloc was cavalier in the way he flung the reality of European Christendom at his contempories. He was constantly saying to them: look at that, you fools, what have you to offer? To achieve success in such an endeavour Belloc had to act the way he did —rough, brutally dogmatic, sweeping in his argument. Muted tones and footnote scholarship can gain skirmishes within the classrooms and the scholarly journals; they have never yet won a large-scale battle. Belloc faced a generation of English journalist-politician intellectuals who looked expectantly to a future grounded on the Whig-Liberal industrialist myth. These were men consciously convinced of the inevitability and the justness of almost every aspect of modern civilization. Belloc swept their case away in book after book, and if the myth of Nordic supremacy is discredited today, if the Catholic ethos and past has something of a hearing in the English-speaking world of our generation, if industrial capitalism is no longer thought to be as natural as the air we breathe and if it is no longer seen as the only alternative to Communism, if the first fifteen centuries of the British Isles are not automatically dismissed by the educated—if the air has changed, it is due in no small measure to that long cavalry charge of Hilaire Belloc, prolonged through fifty years of warfare against what he tersely called "the Barbarians."

A full description of his battle belongs more to a consideration of the man as an historian and as a sociologist. What is to the point here is that what Belloc did grew out of what he was. His heartiness and confidence, his good conscience, sprang from what he *knew* and what he had *seen*. Christendom was something almost physical to him. He assimilated his own past in the most concrete way open to him. He tramped all over Western Europe; he ate much and drank deeply in half-forgotten inns that for him always symbolized roots and freedom; he sailed along the coast of England and charted the landing of the first Normans; he followed the route of the Phoenicians; he knelt before the site of Calvary as an old man. With an iron determination, he willed to become one with all that had gone to make him what he was—a Western Catholic man. In his own home in Sussex he kept alive all the older traditions of the countryside.

It has been said frequently that Belloc remained a stranger in England. Las Vergnas understood him almost exclusively as a Frenchman. He was neither a Frenchman nor an Englishman; he was both of them, and he was more than either of them. In his essays Belloc is a South English peasant and a channel sailor. In his political sympathies, he is an English Monarchist and a French Republican. In the soldierly dimension of himself he is thoroughly Gallic. In his over-all vision, he belongs to the old Roman Empire and to Christendom. He combines within his personality a complexity of cultural and spiritual strains which are never bastardized in any specious internationalism, but which retain their individualities by being welded into an analogous unity by his Catholicism. His was a precarious but happy balance that included the main lines of his blood past and his spiritual antecedents.

If Belloc's over-all historical and cultural perspective is a sweeping thing that encompasses the centuries, it must be remembered that this central principle of historical organization was balanced by a vivid sense of the immediate drama of things past and present. One of the most revealing characteristics of the Bellocian humanism is its lack of academicism—one might almost say its anti-academicism. Belloc is always out on the road with his senses peeled. This psychological fact points up a union of two drives in man which are rarely in harmony with each other: a self-conscious emphasis on the past, and a communion with the physical universe which actually exists.

Traditionalism, when it is espoused by an intelligentsia, frequently suffers from an overdeveloped symbolism. Things are not seen in themselves. They are seen only as symbols. The now is important only to illuminate the past, or to call to mind spiritual and moral values. The purely symbolic always tends to eliminate the concrete, the individual, the existent; it leads the mind through the phenomenal to an eternal which is frequently nothing more than the dust of an abstraction. Several of the great Eastern traditional cultures have atrophied through an overdevelopment of this kind of symbol and mythmaking. Byzantine iconography suffers from it, and insofar as it does, it is not of the West. Carried to the end in the moral order, pure symbolism means that nothing is valued or loved for itself. Philosophically considered, such a tradi-

tionalism is a kind of Platonism in which the world functions only to manifest historical myths or systems of ideas.
If the masses today suffer from a lack of conscious religious,
social and historical symbols, the intellectual suffers from
the contrary: he turns everything solid into a mirror. In-
tellectually this ends in a simple inability to see things as
they are. Theologically, it would appear to be a kind of
subtle Manicheanism, in which nothing is good enough
as it is.

Belloc constantly kept himself engaged with things.
His understanding of the Catholic tradition escapes the
purely symbolic and academic order. What he sees in the
river valleys and inns of Europe *is* symbolic of a great historical effort stamped with the City of God; but what is
so stamped is good in itself. If you would understand the
past that has made you and grasp something of the spirit
of its religion, Belloc urges that you go to Arles, for example; but above all, *see* Arles. Belloc's Grizzlebeard, the
custodian of tradition, is one with his Sailor, the man of
"the five senses."

If his Grizzlebeard were without a Sailor, Belloc's traditionalism would have stiffened into something Egyptian,
mummified. But since he is of the West himself, of an order
which has been eminently practical and concrete as well
as visionary, these two remain one. To exemplify the nature
of tradition, Belloc finds his best instance to be a seaman's
knot.

If his Sailor had had no Grizzlebeard, then Belloc's concrete vision and communion with reality would have degen-
erated into a kind of irrational naturalism. Naturalism is
merely an escape into the physical universe, away from
burdens which are peculiarly human. It is one of the less
healthy offshoots of the fertile tree of Romanticism. Since
no man can just wallow in nature for long without react-

ing in some way, the pure Romantic soon comes up with a view of nature as an irrational force within whose bosom is to be found salvation. The spectacle of D. H. Lawrence comes to mind immediately. The humanist reacts to nature by taming the beast; the Christian humanist tames a Good Beast. But the romantic naturalist attunes himself to the wilderness and finally renounces his social nature. The eighteenth-century City of Man appeared to the early Romantics to be an utter sham. The Age of Reason had run its course, and the intellect had become an intolerable burden. The Romantics tried to escape from their humanity into a physical beyond; having surrendered the reason, they gave themselves up to mythmaking. Mr. Auden has analyzed the peculiar significance of the "sea" and the "desert" for European Romanticism.[33] The "sea" represented the infinite possibilities that urged human nature to break its bond. But this optimism carried within itself the seeds of a subsequent despair. The "desert" represented the possibilities exhausted, the sea dried up. The surrender of the reason and of the corporate wisdom of society ended in giving the spirit over to darkness. The older traditions reminiscent of the Catholic Unity were jettisoned, and the result is known to us all. The *Walpürgis-nacht* orgies under Nazism bore bitter fruit in a cult of blood and soil that just missed wiping out the remnants of Western Christian Europe.

Western man for centuries now has lost the key to his own meaning. He has been striving for a long time to break out of the ruins of a City half destroyed at his own hands. Political Liberalism of the old-fashioned Marxian variety grew out of a psychological desire to get away from where man actually found himself. Post-World War II existentialist despair, considered as a socio-historical reality, is a philosophical justification for this urge to break all existing cultural and historical limits. What must be done, at all costs, is to exorcise our common historical heritage, our faith, our corporate memories. A fresh beginning can be the only beginning. This is a presupposition that is operative everywhere, most concretely in the arts, most consciously in philosophy, and most dangerously in religion.

Such is the estrangement modern man has carved for himself. In social and economic life the masses are estranged from their spiritual and cultural past. Politically, techniques forged by Western man himself have alienated him from his ancient freedom. The home, the nation, the Church, the West, the past, roots, origins—these are always wrong, always wicked: only the wilderness of the future promises salvation. The poet has retreated to that uniquely modern place invented in the early nineteenth century—the state of mind called Bohemia. His destiny seems assured when he has pruned away everything reminiscent of the objective order, and when he finds himself alone with his broken soul. Philosophically, the age has had urged on it the clever monstrosity that since consciousness renders to me what is Other than Myself, then my personality is defined by a negation. Theologically, the Barbarian God of the peat bogs has come back with "neo-orthodoxy," and man is told that he is so utterly other than God that he is in no sense the image of his Creator. The human fabric has been so cut to ribbons that man has been reduced to a nothing that can parade his utter absurdity only by putting on a mask. The clown has come into his own.

Now it is part of the enduring significance of Hilaire Belloc that he saw all of this long ago. He saw it as the enemy of all that Christendom had ever built and loved and believed. He saw it as a unique concentration of evils that separately, one after another, had attacked the Christian City since its inception. He nailed the thing to the wall when he called it the spirit of Barbarism: the spirit that cannot build for itself because it rejects all limit, the essence of finite perfection; the spirit that makes its way in the intellectual world and in that necessary parasite, the world of fashion, by negating all that has gone on before; a spirit that thrives on opposition and rebellion, and that can cheaply dismiss as nothing the common effort of three thousand years.

The Barbarian hopes—and that is the very mark of him—that he can have his cake and eat it too. He will consume what civilization has slowly produced after generations of selection and effort, but he will not be at the pains to replace such goods, nor indeed has he a comprehension of the virtue that has brought them into being. Discipline seems to him irrational, on which account he is ever marvelling that civilization should have offended him with priests and soldiers.

. . . In a word, the Barbarian is discoverable everywhere in this, that he cannot *make;* that he can befog and destroy, but that he cannot sustain; and of every Barbarian in the decline or peril of every civilization exactly that has been true.[34]

Belloc is one of the few writers in the English world of the last fifty years who wanted to remain himself, and who desired to stand exactly where he was: a Christian man standing in a tradition whose religion is Catholic and whose origins are in the Roman Order. Because of this, Belloc will never be considered an Intellectual. He should not be so considered. He detested the term. The contemporary Intellectual of the Western World has come out of the same past as Belloc, but he rejects that past as he rejects its religion. That is why the past fifty to seventy-five years of intellectual life have been fevered with experiment—in literature, in philosophy, in politics, in all the arts, and in morals. If some new truth has emerged from it all, and if some beauty has been etched in the darkness, does it not seem as nothing to what has been given up?

Christopher Dawson stated once that the modern soul is at bottom anti-ontological. It hates being. Hilaire Belloc has said that the modern soul hates proportion and limitation. They are both affirming the same truth, because the condition of all being save God is limitation. Integrated Christian humanism accepts the finite goodness that constitutes the nature of man. Out of this affirmation the soul can build of itself a work of art; without this affirmation, man gives himself over to the darkness in the suicide of self-alienation.

We sit by and watch the Barbarian, we tolerate him; in the long stretches of peace we are not afraid.
We are tickled by his irreverence, his comic inversion of our old certitudes and our fixed creeds refreshes us; we laugh. But as we laugh we are watched by large and awful faces from beyond: and on these faces there is no smile.[35]

These faces are masks of that one Evil that has ever enticed man into the wilderness. Belloc the soldier saw it riding out of the Eastern wastes, trampling under the vine-yards and desecrating the shrines of Christian men, giving over the soil to the sands and the mind to an awful simplicity. He saw it rising within the great Universities of Europe, rubbing out the certitudes and the songs of Catholic Men.

His soul too had been wounded by the darkness that surrounds the spirit and makes for isolation. There is a passage in *Esto Perpetua* in which Belloc—once again "Myself"—met a stranger in Timgad, that African town, once Roman and fertile, now empty and given back to the desert. They spoke to one another, and their conversation was the drama of salvation and damnation. Belloc looked on the desert, and he was tempted: the soul seemed nothing, and he thought of those who "see at last that there is no Person in destiny, and that purpose is only in themselves. Their

Faiths turn to legend, and at last they enter that shrine whose God has departed and whose Idol is quite blind."[36] He felt terror and was less a man. But he turned and went back to the place he had known, and the terror left him, and he was a man once again.

Chapter Two

GRIZZLEBEARD:
HISTORY FROM WITHIN

Among all the disciplines in which Hilaire Belloc has laboured, history stands out as his most ambitious field of endeavour. Belloc's historical *practice* is too complex to be judged in any general essay concerning his essential importance. But his historical *theory* is crucially important for fixing the limits of his integrated Christian humanism. It is as an extension of his humanism that his historical position will be analyzed.

The cardinal significance of the Bellocian conception of history is its traditionalism. History is organic; it grows from within a culture and is the actual cause of that culture's corporate existence in present time. Since Christendom has been rendered one by a religious tradition that has permeated the diverse dimensions of the past—familial, regional, and the rest—the past is rendered intelligible by grasping the inner spirit that has seeded the ground and watered the growth of historical man. Those who attack Hilaire Belloc for being biased in his historical perspective must first settle the question of the very nature of history itself. For Belloc history begins as an extension of tradition; history is an act of "self-knowledge," as he puts it in his magnificent introduction to *Europe and the Faith.*

This act of self-knowledge does not proceed from any desire to systematize or catalogue facts. It does not proceed from the need man has for the possession of impersonal, objective truth. History is the effect of an inner command to know one's soul. It is the completion of human consciousness. The passion for history is man's Grizzlebeard. As the Sailor renders Myself unalienated from the physical universe in which he exists, the Grizzlebeard seals Myself in time which has stamped man in its own image. Belloc returns to this theme time and again in the essays, but nowhere does he express himself more movingly than in *The Old Road*, where he tells us why he elected to recover the Roman Way from Winchester to Canterbury.

> To study something of great age until one grows familiar with it and almost to live in its time, is not merely to satisfy a curiosity or to establish aimless truths: it is rather a function whose appetite has always rendered History a necessity. By the recovery of the Past, stuff and being are added to us; our lives, which, lived in the present only, are a film or surface, take on body—are lifted into one dimension more. The soul is fed. Reverence and knowledge and security and the love of a good land—all these are increased or given by the pursuit of this kind of learning. Visions or intimations are confirmed . . . One may say that historical learning grants men glimpses of life completed and a whole; and such a vision should be the chief solace of whatever is mortal and cut off imperfectly from fulfillment.[37]

It is well known that the humanist conception of history as a psychological necessity first came into its own in the Western World with the Incarnation of the Son of God in time. In the classical pagan world the status of history was at best ambiguous. Aristotle gave historical knowledge a low place in his hierarchy of values. History for the Greek philosophers could not achieve the dignity of a science because it lacked the universal necessity without which there is no science. The philosophers were right in judging history not to be a science. They were wrong in according history little value. What the wise men of the ancient world took away from history, the common sense of the people gave back. The dignity of history was grasped obscurely because the humanism of the classical universe could not achieve its fullness unless man was unified in time as well as in space. The tradition of the family enshrined in the household gods and in the legend of Aeneas carrying father Anchises on his back out of burning Troy symbolized a need rooted in the substance of human nature: the necessity to link the present with the past. Familial traditions extended to the City, and then to the Empire, and even the work of Virgil the Poet was historical in inspiration.

The Incarnation in time and the prolonging of the Deposit of Faith through the centuries in a living tradition that hands on what it has received, confirmed the humanist insight and at the same time conferred on history a dignity of an altogether new order. No one in the new Christian society, not even the scientist or philosopher, would ever more despise history, and if the West has accorded to history a place unique in the hierarchy of human values, it is because time had been sanctified and conquered by the Son of God.

History added to classical man a depth he needed in order to be himself. The Faith taught Christian man that nothing is ever lost: the ages themselves live a timeless and ever fresh life in the Vision of God. Tradition, which is nothing but the corporate life of the past existing in the present, is the human analogue of the Eternal Morning Who is the End of us all.

Historical tradition, to grow as it should, must commence with that society which is most natural to man: the family. Familial memory incarnated in a host of rites, observances, and actions lifts the members of this primordial community out of the impermanence of a present ever passing, and life is invested with a fullness that the immortal in man demands. The moment is salvaged, and the suffering and estrangement forced on humanity by the sheer duty of living becomes:

> . . . part of a large business which may lead to Beatitude . . . Not only death (which shakes and rends all that is human in us, creating a monstrous separation and threatening the soul with isolation which destroys), not only death, but that accompaniment of mortality which is a perpetual series of lesser deaths and is called change, is challenged, chained, and put in its place by unaltered and successive acts of seasonable regard for loss and dereliction and mutability.[38]

This immemorial *sense* for history has always run through every artery of the corporate life of Christendom, and in Hilaire Belloc it finds a final champion. Read *A Remaining Christmas* or *The Mowing of a Field* for an insight into Belloc's sense of history as tradition. For him, and here he is one with that past he claimed for himself, history is simply the recovery of the self: a personal and communal act of memory. For Belloc, as for the West, tradition begins in the family: the Yule log was burnt in his home. From the family, tradition spread to the region: he rendered Sussex immortal. From the region, man recovers those wider circles of his story—the nation, the state, the broad sweep of the Empire: some forty books enshrine the Bellocian effort. All of this is finally stamped one by the Faith that issued from the Incarnation.

Belloc's historical work is divided broadly into two chief fields of interest: England and France; and within these respective areas of concentration a particular era predominates: in England it is the Reformation, down to the final exile of the Stuart Kings; in France, it is the Revolution and the Napoleonic Empire. Transcending these broad in-

terests, there are works which deal with the wider sweep
of Western History from before the Incarnation, down
through the Middle Ages, up to the Reformation and
even beyond World War I to the *Crisis of Our Civilization*.
Biography and general history incarnate the above work.
Besides all that, Belloc has produced an odd dozen special-
ized monographs which deal with subjects close to his
heart: studies on the Roman Road, on Sussex, on cities and
their river tributaries, and finally on military history. The
first two attach to his general European history and illustrate his "pro-Roman" and "pro-Catholic" positions. The
military monographs are grouped chiefly, although not
exclusively, around England. Not including his travel
books, which illustrate historical matter, one can count
forty-six books written by Belloc that are historical in the
full sense of the term.

The story of Belloc's going up to Oxford as an under-
graduate, astounding the University with his brilliance
and pugnacity, is well known. The story of his exclusion
from Oxford as a tutor because of his bellicose Catholicism
may be revealed some day. In any case, this rebuff added
something personal to his bitterness against what he called
the "official history" of the great English Universities.
His work must be understood in relation to the two historical trends that he reacted against with such violence:
the Whig tradition of Gibbon, Mommsen, Macaulay,
Green, and their copyists and sycophants; and the implicit
idealism and anti-traditionalism of German *Historismus*.
Because he was engaged in a conscious and articulate controversy with these two historical schools for almost fifty
years, an understanding of what he is opposing is indis-
pensable for placing Belloc as an historian.

Present-day English history has maintained a steady, un-
broken continuity with eighteenth-century political Whig-

gery and eighteenth-century rationalism. History was an admirable tool for the elucidation of doctrines peculiarly dear to the whole Enlightenment (as Voltaire so clearly grasped). The indefinite perfectibility of human reason could be illustrated historically by showing the advance of man out of medieval darkness into the light of the Age of Reason. Here the specific dogmas of rationalist deism *happened* to coincide with the prejudices of popular Protestantism: that the Church was foisted on an unwilling Empire at the caprice of Constantine the Great; that the barbarian hordes from the east swept over the body of Rome and breathed a new life into Europe that flowered eventually in a host of Protestant institutions; that the Dark Ages extended into the high Middle Ages and were expelled only by the advent of the Renaissance of learning (executed, if not initiated by scholars freed from the tyranny of Rome); that the growth of Parliamentary Government in Holland and England was the work of disinterested patriots forging a future freed from feudal darkness and oppression—all these opinions, dear to the traditions of the Glorious Revolution, were simply corollaries of the rationalist doctrine of the expanding perfection of mankind. Darwinism was only a latter-day confirmation of this ideology. From Protestant opinion and rationalist philosophy was born the thing known as Whig History. The eighteenth- and nineteenth-century Whig-rationalist was dead certain that he had in his hands the guide lines to historical understanding. It seems significant that even old-line Tories who politically opposed the bulk of the Whig-Liberal traditions fell into the general Whig position. Bolingbroke himself was a victim of pre-Darwinian evolutionism.

Since man was supposed to have *progressed* to that point in time where the historian stood, history was judged from the vantage point of the present. Everything from before Christ, down to the decline of the Roman Empire, the Dark and Middle Ages, through the Renaissance and be- yond the Reformation was measured by standards peculiar to the present. The past received its intelligibility in the light of where man happened to find himself. All this fol- lowed on a doctrine of inevitable progress. Since the pres- ent was the high point of cultural and personal develop- ment, the past was considered ministerially. Our fathers were condescended to.

Now it is extremely significant that Hilaire Belloc, almost alone of his Edwardian generation, reversed that historical perspective. He called before the bar of Christendom the capitalist, industrialist present, and found it wanting. Belloc insisted on judging the present in the light of the past, and the past itself was seen in terms of *its* own immediate and remote antecedents. The reality of the European traditions of individual freedom and proprietary justice, the very being of cultural historical continuity, entered bodily into his perspective. Whereas the Whig historian judged King Charles I, to take an obvious example, in the light of the twentieth-century development to liberal parliamentary government, Belloc saw the man in terms of the ancient traditions of popular monarchy within the law for which the Stuart monarch died. Cromwell, for the Whig histor- ian, was he who made for parliamentary supremacy; for Belloc, Cromwell was he who was made by an aristocracy swollen with the wealth of the religious revolution.

Since Belloc's conception of history is traditional and organic, he constantly insisted on judging the past in the light of the lines of efficient causality that were actually pro- ductive of this or that historical event or crisis. These lines are many and diverse, but at least one of them, Belloc in- sists, renders European history a steady continuity. This line of causality is the Catholic and Greco-Roman classical tradition; an almost immemorial tradition existing in the present in two dimensions: corporately—in Christendom as a whole, molding it by shaping institutions, forming consciences, transforming the land, incarnating the hopes of generations of men in the visual and literary arts, and handing on the religious heritage to the unborn; and personally—as summing itself up in a man, annealing him, and giving direction to his destiny.

In taking his historical stand on the Catholic tradition, Belloc was fitting his historical judgment to a reality that had been, and although radically attenuated still was, the one bond of continuity that could enable the historian to grasp a steady, continuous causality in his province. The Whig doctrines were myths, but even assuming for a moment that the late nineteenth and early twentieth centuries were superior to the Medieval and Continental traditions— that the present was the threshold to a golden age, as the Victorians and Edwardians still thought—nonetheless, that supposition was completely valueless as a principle of historical explanation.

The Whig historian and his Liberal counterpart attempt to find some intelligibility or meaning in history. The rejection of the Catholic ethos robs the Whig of the one steady, continuous influence that has always operated in the West through the ages. The Whig cannot, for example, see the rise of liberty as something caused by the Faith, as an *effect* of an institution already in existence. His dilemma consists in seeing a genuine growth in liberty; his rejection of the Catholic tradition forces him to one of two alternatives: either liberty is purely fortuitous and has no over-all historical cause, and history is thereby totally unintelligible; or liberty is the effect of something not actually in existence, but which is conceived as though it were. From the

latter issues the Liberal-Whig mythology of "progress,"
"evolution," "human perfectibility," and so on. What these
historians seem incapable of understanding is that these
formulas stand for nothing but tissues of imagery, existing
in the minds of men who view historical situations after
the fact. In no sense did "progress" ever cause anything
historical, for the simple reason that "progress" *has no
being* of its own. Yet the Liberals treat these constructs
as though they were physical laws operative in the extra-
mental order. Belloc had more than a lively grip on this
fallacy, and he fingered it for the imaginative trick it is,
in his controversy with H. G. Wells.

> When Mr. Wells concludes this passage by saying "I strut to
> no such personal beatitude," and then goes on to say, "the life
> to which I belong uses me and will go on beyond me, and I am
> content," he does two unintelligent things. First of all, he mixes
> up the real with the imaginary . . . and next he falls into the
> very common error of confused intellects—the personification
> of abstract ideas. "The life to which we belong uses us" is a
> meaningless phrase. God may use us or we may use ourselves,
> or some other third Will, not God's or our own, may use us:
> but "the life to which we belong" does not use us. Talking like
> that is harmless when it is mere metaphor, it is asinine when it
> sets up to be definition.[39]

Wells was not alone in this personification of the abstract. He was only a popularizer of a tendency that is ever
at work in all historical theory that commences by mini-
mizing the religious causality operative in the West. The
Whig substituted for the Catholic tradition an over-all
finality which he called "progress." The idealist historian
and the *Weltanschauung* historian add to the Whig denial
the negation of the personal will. All the historian is left
to work with are impersonal forces, either physical or
logical. He falls into the old error of laying his eggs in a
basket that does not exist.

The Liberal is bound by his own theory. His sociological ideals must be projected ahead of his historical understanding; they can never emerge from an insight into that which actually has existed. The classical European Liberal (and his contemporary counterpart) is always marked by his rejection of any way of life rooted in the older past of Christendom.

When Hilaire Belloc launched his concept of the proprietary state, he effected a political and sociological revolution that had its roots in his historical vision. Mr. Douglas Jerrold has analyzed brilliantly the profound effect made by Belloc's polemic against the English parliamentary party system which was wedded to Whig ideals and their Edwardian Liberal refinements.[40] It was a time when Britain had reached next to the limit of its material expansion. English industry and productivity were unequalled in excellence and quantity. The nation was united in the firm conviction that Britannia ruled by the grace of God. Providence had specially blessed the Island Empire. The innate superiority, not only of Englishmen, but of English ways and English religion, was less a conscious doctrine than a broad myth on which a whole people reposed. Liberal capitalism appeared to the "progressivists" as the final flowering of a history that had its roots in the Reformation and the Glorious Revolution of 1688.

Belloc's economics and sociology, the fruit of his historical insight, effected a revolution. Since it was a revolution of thought, its effects were not immediately apparent, but acting as corrosives they gradually ate away the rust of centuries of complacency and smugness. Belloc told the Englishmen of his day that their cherished system of parliamentary government represented not the nation, but two parties that stood for the same thing: capitalist, industrial wealth. He went on to tell them that the supposed incorruptibility of this ancient governmental institution was a lie: men were bought and sold, and titles were bartered for privilege.

Expanding his polemic, Belloc informed the nation that liberal capitalism would not issue into the golden age, but would work inexorably toward the Servile State: a state in which the vast majority of the populace laboured perforce for a small minority of wealthy owners, or for an entrenched government dominated by technical experts. He grounded his predictions on the drying up of the traditional economic basis of Western Christian societies: the institution of small property, widely distributed, giving the tone to society, and reposing on the family community. As far back as 1908, in *The Servile State*, Belloc deduced that unless the institution of property were reestablished, the nation would give itself over to slavery. The England of the late forties and early fifties has borne him out with tragic finality. Belloc contended that party control was an irrelevant point; if the society were propertyless, contractual slavery would inexorably result. The age of the ration card, the social leveling of the whole people, the increasing drabness of life, the elimination of the middle classes, the legislation of enforced labour—this age is upon England, and it will remain until and unless property is restored.

Belloc's prophecies were successes in the only way any prophecy can succeed. What he said would come to pass did come to pass; and it came to pass the way he said it would. There is more than irony in looking back thirty years to that superman of the Wells school of thought: that uninhibited, traditionless blank who was to be the term of the march of liberal progress; that dull abstraction, "the man of the future," who was to inherit the earth. Who is he today, and where is he? He is the industrial

slave of an impoverished and spiritually bankrupt Europe—
Heidegger's faceless "one" who neither owns nor can be
said even to be.

The striking truth in the utter failure of the hopes of
post-Victorian Liberalism lies in the fact that Liberalism,
the child of Whiggery, grounded its predictions in an historical theory that was a well-intentioned myth. The future
simply is not a magnet. It has no existence. It is a refuge
for cowards, Chesterton said somewhere; a retreat for men
who cannot bear to face the grandeur of their own past.
Belloc was able to lay down the broad lines which were
leading to the Servile State because his historical vision was
orientated realistically: it looked to causes actually operative in the past, whose collective efficacy hardened and
sharpened with the passing of time. The English Reformation had created a wealthy landed aristocracy. This aristocracy had ruined a crown that for all its failures had
stood, immemorially, for the rights of the common man,
already a landed owner in large part by the close of the
fourteenth century. Having gained political power, the
aristocracy usurped economic power; the long series of
legislative acts and judicial decisions, from the Poor Laws
to the final enclosure acts, ended in the creation of a rural
proletariat. The rise of industrialism was controlled by a
capitalism already in existence, and the rural proletariat was
transformed into its urban counterpart.

Belloc's prophetic ability, strikingly demonstrated time
and again, worked because it was based on his grasp of
causality actually operative in history. The future can
never be predicted with certitude because causes operating
at the present moment in time are contingent. They can be
replaced, diminished, checked, or rechannelled. Nonetheless, to have an insight into these causes is to possess an
instrument for predicting a possible or even probable

future. No historical theory grounded in a mere *Weltan-schauung*, nor any history deduced from a philosophical system such as the Hegelian and Marxist, is of any practical utility in understanding what might happen.

Another example of Belloc's prophetic insight can be found in his book about the United States, *The Contrast*. Writing in 1924, before the New Deal was even a dream, Belloc calmly announced that a great increase of Presidential power would be effected in the near future. His historical thesis, still paradoxical to most of his readers, was that great wealth always operated through representative institutions, and always aimed, neither at monarchy nor democracy, but at aristocracy. In a country in which the sense of individual liberty was still strong, the people would tend to incarnate themselves more and more in the head of the state, who, by his very position, stood above special interests, which worked naturally through parliamentary structures. One does not have to agree with Belloc that this monarchical tendency was a good thing; but it must be granted that he nailed the tendency to the wall.

Belloc's historical insight passes the pragmatic test time and again. Another example of history rendered intelligible when seen in the light of the traditions of Christendom was Belloc's very early penetration of the essential foreignness of Prussia to the family of nations that constitute Europe. Prussia, the legitimate child of the Reformation, arose and developed apart from the older European Unity. Of her very nature she opposed that unity, and refused to be bound by the morality common to Christian nations and men. Frederick the Great's rape of Silesia, the work of Bismarck, the over-all meaning of the First Reich and of World War I make sense only within the context of Belloc's discussion of the problem. When all England and the United States as well were singing the praises of the Nordic

man and the superiority of the blond beast of the north,
Belloc knew what Prussia really meant: a gun pointed at the
heart of the West. The resurrection of Prussianism under
Hitler confirmed bitterly the prophetic insight of Belloc,
who had been warning England for over forty years about
the intentions of North Germany. Belloc knew where
Prussia stood in the light of the unity of Christendom. She
was beyond the pale.

It is largely due to the Bellocian polemic that the old-
fashioned Whig history, although still taught as a matter
of course almost everywhere, is no longer the accepted
dogma of serious historical scholarship. Historians today
can labour at their profession without the fear that their
work will be branded as partisan, as is the work of the man
who cleared the field for them.

Belloc's historical technique suffered from one self-im-
posed liability. He worked within a tradition, and thereby
defined himself. But his strength lay in his very limitation.
The Bellocian philosophy of history can operate only
within some one well-defined civilization. The effectiveness
of his method depends on the historian's entering profoundly into the spirit of a culture, and on assuming to
himself the religious and social beliefs and values of the
society in question. Without his Catholicism, or without
at least a deep sympathy for the religion that made Christendom, Belloc's historical method cannot be made to func-
tion realistically. It is of no use, for example, to a man who
would work toward an historical understanding of global
history. World history must be seen, to the Bellocian, as
something outside of the European Unity, as something
foreign, threatening that unity, or as penetrated by it. To
enter into a diversity of religious and cultural traditions in
order to grasp the complete picture of world history *from
within* is a psychological impossibility. A man would break

down under the strain, because he cannot take to himself traditions that are mutually contradictory. He cannot be that which he rejects.

Philosophies of world history always wear that curious air of unreality typified by academic journals or international youth congresses. So long as these historians simply record facts they are safe, but as soon as they attempt explanations they break down because of their necessary lack of inside understanding. World historians frequently fail to grasp even the story of their own nations. They are within nothing at all, but are self-estranged cultural strangers looking at the world from an academic outside; hence they fail to grasp the spirit of anything that has ever moved men to common action. These historians tend to succumb to the facile temptation of writing history synthetically; they perpetually find meetings between an East and West, where there is only conflict; they fall into the trap of treating history cyclically; they build vast structures in the air that reveal nothing to a man searching for his own antecedents. A Christian comes away from Belloc knowing his own soul.

The *Weltanschauung* historian must fail in the end because no "world view" has ever acted to cause anything historically. History is caused within cultures, and the clash of civilizations occurs when two cultures in act meet on the field of battle, be it economic, military, or spiritual.

The final objection that the "world historian" has against Belloc is that he takes sides, and the final answer to that objection is simply this: to refuse to take sides is to refuse to enter history. A historian who does not see that rather brutal fact will never see more than the surface of things. He cannot see the inside of the spiritual drama of, let us say, the Reformation or the Arian heresy, without being touched by an absolute: absolutes either wound or enlist the assent of the spirit. There can be no impartiality when a man has been actually grazed by the realities that have stirred all Christianity to its roots. Intellectual aloofness to the issues of life and death simply demonstrates that these frontiers of the soul have not been reached by the historian, and unless they are reached and elected for or rejected, nothing historical can be known in its very substance. *Credo ut intelligam.*

Now then, so it is with us who are of the Faith and the great story of Europe. A Catholic as he reads that story does not grope at it from without, he understands it from within . . . he is also that which he has to understand. The Faith is Europe and Europe is the Faith.

The Catholic brings to history (when I say "history" in these pages I mean the history of Christendom) self-knowledge. As a man in the confessional accuses himself of what he knows to be true, and what other people cannot judge, so a Catholic, talking of the united European civilization, when he blames it, blames it for motives and for acts which are his own. He himself could have done those things in person. He is not relatively right in this blame, he is absolutely right. As a man can testify to his own motive, so can the Catholic testify to unjust, irrelevant, or ignorant conceptions of the European story; for he knows why and how it proceeded. Others, not Catholic, look upon the story of Europe externally as strangers. *They* have to deal with something which presents itself to them partially and disconnectedly, by its phenomena alone: *he* sees it all from its centre in its essence, and together.

I say again, renewing the terms, The Church is Europe: and Europe is the Church.[41]

The Bellocian concept of history, as set forth in the above passage, might well be called Anselmian: historical understanding follows Faith. If history is an extension of a complex line of traditions unified through a common religion, then it follows necessarily that history can be grasped only from within. The historian who views the

European story as a series of "phenomena" external to himself must either fall into the Aristotelian conception of history as mere chronology, or he must superimpose on this series some conceptual framework to render it intelligible. He simply cannot enter into its spirit and see with the eyes of the men he would know, or feel with them as they erupt into common action. He is alienated from them.

Belloc has been attacked by historians, both Catholic and non-Catholic, for partisanship, bias, and narrow dogmatism. There is more than a little truth to their charges. Belloc frequently bludgeons his readers. In the later books he forces them into line with a prose that is almost martial in its proud magnificence: its certainty. But all this is part of the price Belloc had to pay to become the kind of historian he did. He is within what he is writing. Do not ask for impartiality when reading of the First Crusade. Belloc is there: he is one of the Crusaders. When you know Belloc, you know the Crusades, you know the revolutionary spirit that swept all France in the eighteenth century; when you have read *Esto Perpetua* the grandeur of the first three centuries of the Christian era comes home to the soul amidst the contrast of the barren desert of Islam. You understand what Islam meant to Europe. Belloc gives a reader a one-sided history, but the irony is that, to a Bellocian, history must always be one-sided. The man "on no side" is outside history.

Paradoxically enough, Belloc's contention runs exactly contrary to the first principle of modern Western historical theory. Contemporary historians, regardless of political predilection or religious and philosophical adherence, are united in the common belief that historical truth is dependent on historical "objectivity." This objectivity is achieved in proportion to the historian's ability to withdraw from his own cultural antecedents. In so doing, the

scholar shakes himself loose from the prejudices and pa-
rochialisms of his own civilization, he frees himself, in
order that he may view the whole. The story of his people
and of his own faith recede until they take their just place
within the broader scope of the cosmic movement of historical man through time.

It is questionable whether such an objectivity can be
more than an ideal projected before the historian—a goal
to be forever missed, but always aimed at. But assuming
for a moment that it is possible for a single historian to
hold before himself the global passage of man through
recorded history, assuming that he could find a set of
natural principles that would unify this vast procession of
phenomena into an intelligible structure—even assuming
this ideal of the Toynbee school of thought—it still remains
an open question whether this would constitute the possession of historical *truth*.

If, on the contrary (assuming Belloc's hypothesis), historical truth principally means historical *understanding* of
the men who have made history, then this understanding
can only follow on a grasp of the spiritual tides that have
launched any given culture, that have given it a common
destiny, that have been channelled analogically through
the members of the community. Historical truth depends
then on a subjective, almost intuitive, grasp of this communal spirit; a penetration into historical man, rather than
an analytic dissection of a spirit that defies mere logical
analysis. Historical understanding escapes the kind of objectivity achieved in the sciences, because it demands a
deeper insight: an entering into the subjective engagement
of the human person. To understand what has caused me
to be the kind of man I am, I must understand what caused
the men who made me to be what they were. I possess my
past, in Belloc's eyes, when I am that past to such a degree

that I could have acted as did my ancestors. Then, and only then, do I actually know my own fathers from within the depths of my own personality.

Outside objectivity versus inside understanding; conscious withdrawal and deliberate cultural alienation for the sake of objectivity, as opposed to conscious cultural immersion and integration for the sake of subjective sympathy: two theories of history that can be resolved finally only by a personal act of choice.

Belloc's historical theory is anti-academic in that it cannot be achieved within the confines of the world of the university. As both an historical position and an historical practice it must always be suspect to professional historical scholars, whose almost exclusive preoccupation with *documents* makes them, quite naturally, more sympathetic to the scientific objectivity of contemporary history. Belloc must always appear, by turns, wildly romantic and narrowly partisan to the academicians. To the Bellocian, academicism in history must always lack both colour and vigour. It must wear an air of irritating professionalism.

Belloc's position absolutely necessitated his emphasis on travel, his minute detection of physical details, his sympathy with verbal tradition, his suspicion for the "outlander." These were all humanistic instruments, rendering him one with the past, capable of seeing things as did his forefathers, understanding reality as they did, and eventually grasping the inner spirit of their personal and communal action that constitutes the heart of their history.

Such history is both conservative in ultimate judgment and it is radical: conservative in that it proceeds by way of a personal guarding of an ancient heritage; radical in that it makes a man totally opposed to a new world at odds with that heritage. The final and the fatal limitation to Bellocian history is that it depends for success on a constant living continuity, on a vital tradition acting like a road the historian can travel down and back again at will. The radical discontinuity of the modern world with its past in the older Christendom makes it almost impossible for anyone to perpetuate Belloc's historical practice. It is becoming increasingly more difficult, if not impossible, *to be* spiritually and affectively one with our heritage. The past of Christendom is becoming more and more a written patrimony, and the Bellocian brand of historical integration cannot thrive on such jejune food.

History by way of inside understanding is practicable today only on a regional and familial basis; and even the family, within the industrialized world, has lost any living touch with its own dead. The father has become a stranger to his son.

For Belloc, therefore, an apprehension of the European past demands an understanding and a sympathy for the Catholic Faith, tending to allegiance, if not to formal profession. As Belloc sees it, only such an history can comprehend the over-all pressure of the Christian dispensation as it exercised a steady influence on the person and on society; acting always as a balm, sometimes as a force, both conservative and full of ringing affirmations that are not of this world. Nonetheless, Belloc affirms, this apprehension is of itself sufficient to insure only an over-all sane judgment about things historical. The Christian vision, to perfect itself historically, must take on a judgment that is temporal, human, and almost cynical in its realism. The great Action advances or retreats as it is involved in the individual actions of ages, generations, decades, and even days and hours. These, in their turn, are caused by a host of agents, tangling one with another, clashing in opposition and uniting in the coincidence of common interest: causes which are both impersonal and personal, but chiefly the latter.

The historian, says Belloc, must possess himself of a mass of detailed impersonal information, which must be sifted and fitted into proper perspective. "But if he is not seized of the mind which lay behind all that was human in the business, then no synthesis of his detailed knowledge is possible."[42] In short, as Mr. Robert Hamilton pointed out in his study on Belloc, the historian must be a humanist. He must understand men and the motives that move them. History, to be faithful to what was actually productive of the past, must go beyond the physical, phenomenal evidence at hand. A judgment of motive will normally transcend the synthesis of observable fact. A man of action (unless he be a Communist) does not give himself away on paper. His motives must be inferred from the way he acts. A detailed observation of a man's conduct over a period of time and through a succession of historical crises will yield sufficient evidence for an over-all judgment as to his intentions, and hence to his place in the historical drama in which he was engaged. No one piece of information is sufficient for such an evaluation. The sum of facts, considered separately, would yield only probability concerning the directed human will. The information as synthesized, however, permits of an inductive judgment yielding a species of certitude about the moral role men play in history. In *The Cruise of the Nona*, that mosaic of Bellociana, the theory is put forth by the author that a sum of probabilities can furnish certitude, if that sum is taken as a patterned whole. It looks as though Belloc is here reflecting the influence of his early teacher, John Henry Newman, who developed an epistemology around this conception of certitude as emerging from a set of probabilities. When all the evidence together points to one conclusion, converges on one exclusive explanation, then the mind should assent to that one conclusion without fear of the truth of the opposite. It is clear that this is a risky and dangerous instrument for the acquisition of historical truth. A fool, or a mind purely speculative or deductive in bent, would bungle in attempting such judgments. A mind overly pious and overly sanguine about human nature, or excessively cynical about the good in men, would not be suited for the task. It is an instrument for a humanist: a man who knows men as they are. Belloc was peculiarly capable of exercising his own theory, and if he erred sometimes, it was on the side of cynicism, not piety.

Belloc's theory of history is not developed philosophically in any one piece of writing. He tosses out his ideas within the limits of short personal essays, and occasionally he illuminates what he is doing in some concrete situation by standing back, as it were, and reflecting briefly on the presuppositions guiding his reasoning. He wrote history *analogically*, and if he had thoroughly developed his doctrine theoretically, he would have revealed something unique in the philosophy of historical practice. Historical research, if it would conform itself with historical truth, must be analogical as is historical truth itself. A diversity of causal lines, one at least almost immemorial, others lengthening into centuries, and still others contracted within the space of a man's life or within a lesser temporal span, all act together to produce history, but each causal line acts in its own way. The historian must constantly shift his perspective as he makes his way through this tangle of actualities, which encompass everything from a living Faith, through the whole gamut of human vice and honour, to the half-forgotten contours of the field of battle. No one factor *determines* history (although one factor—the Christian Greco-Roman tradition—renders history *intelligible*). Herein Belloc is consciously separated from Marxist history, which would explain the past as determined exclusively through economic pressures. Even more so is the Bellocian theory opposed to the Hegelian or dialectical concept of history in which the past is judged to be caused by a logical clash of ideas which work themselves out in time, independently of, or dominating, the counter-pressure of human action.

To study, think, and write history as Belloc did demands a rare brand of personal integration. A personal Faith, through which the Christian tradition is comprehended, is united with humanism, through which the human and non-human causes operative in history are accorded their just causality in the judgment of the past. These lines of causality must be kept distinct, but they cannot be separated. If they are separated, the historian will fall into some kind of Barthianism, in which the Gospel is conceived as a message that acts through the ages independently of men and society, and in which secular man goes his own way totally uneffected by the Christian dispensation. If, on the contrary, the lines of causality are identified, then history is turned into the pious hagiography of fashionable French ladies of the last century. To ignore or to minimize either the Church or the secular is to fail to understand Western Europe.

As an example of Belloc's balancing of historical causality one should watch him in act as he analyzes the French Revolution. A host of causes made the Revolution: the Christian doctrine of human equality; the ruining of the prestige of the monarchy by Louis XV's public indulgence of the flesh prolonged into middle and old age; the antiquated system of taxation, based on a defunct manorial society, which bankrupted the realm; the extravagance and scandal given by a woman too long denied the rights of marriage; Drouet's ride ("Good Lord, what a ride!" says Belloc); the heroism of the French at Wattignies; the democratic spirit of the Gauls united so paradoxically with the temper of the soldier—these were all actual causes of the Revolution. The failure of almost any one of them would have ruined or at least modified the Revolution.

When faced with these facts, few historians would deny the rightness of Belloc's contention. But it remains true that these causes, all of which moved to one effect, are not actually operative within the minds of most academic historians when they set down the story. What use would an Hegelian have for that splendid ride that headed off the flight of the King? His theory cannot admit that wild contingency, full of the drama of human existence, to have altered the course of history. He is bound by his own dialectic. Neither the free will of Drouet, nor the strength of the man's horse, nor the quality of his skill, can genuinely enter Hegelian history; nor can they enter the systems of Spengler and those contemporary historians influenced by him, because *systems* of constructs cannot admit of the drama of historical contingency. What modern vulgarian, conditioned by our mechanical theories about sex, can *really* understand Marie Antoinette—so Catholic at the end, and always so much the woman! Theories of history can take these contingencies and admit them as *facts*, but they can not use them in their over-all explanations. These historians are not humanists, but are men who would like to be scientists in a realm that escapes the purely scientific.

For an insight into Belloc's humanist penetration, one could do little better than to read him on King Charles I of England. For centuries Charles has been a puzzle to students of history: carrying with him all the glamour of the Stuarts, he was certainly the noblest of that ill-omened house (if one except James Francis Edward), and yet why did he let Strafford go to his death? This moral failure of the King is contradicted by his heroism through the whole civil war, from the raising of the royal standard at Nottingham to his execution. Charles simply does not look like a well-intentioned weakling: we cannot think of him as a coward at one instant and a hero at the next; there is a constancy about his whole life, and how can this constancy be understood in the light of the death of Strafford? Explained it must be, if the English Civil War is to make sense. Belloc, uniting the Newmanian technique of converging probabilities with the insight of a humanist, draws this sketch of the man's character:

I may compare the effects of his inward strength to the effects produced by one kind of resistance against an impact.

When men plan to make impact against resistance in the will of another they expect, and commonly find, at first a resistance. They proceed to wear it down. If it gets less, they are introduced to a last struggle in which, when they have taken all the outworks, they may naturally expect to succeed. So it was with the pressure brought against the boy's father, James I, in the first beginnings of the revolt of the gentry against him. James' Parliaments—that is, the country gentlemen—pushed him further and further. Such an action is like a siege, it can have but one end, and as we know, James, fighting from trench to trench, always, in the end, gave way.

Then again, there is the kind of resistance offered by men who are adamant in the beginning. They bluntly refuse, and if you lose your first battle against them you can go no further.

But Charles was to be neither of these. His nature, trained in isolation, was fluid against the first onset of attack; then there came a moment when the attack reached something quite different from the first fluid resistance—a stone wall. It was thus that he came to his death. Men were led on to think him pliable; when they came unexpectedly on rigidity, they were infuriated.

Now this distinction, I take it, between his fixity upon certain things, well defined in his own mind, and his indecision or rather lack of convinced *cause* for resistance on the rest—this quality in him which kept in reserve and hidden an ultimate power of complete refusal (even to martyrdom) took root, I say, in these very early years when he was compelled, almost against himself, to consider in private what remedy he could find for his defects.[43]

Belloc did not find the above in any written document, admitting of a learned footnote. He concluded to it, following on a study of all the available data. His moral judgment concerning Charles would be called "romancing" by historians of one brand of the *Historismus* school. If history is but surface phenomena or ideology, then these men are right. But if history has been *caused* efficiently, in part, by men acting in all their strength and failing in their weaknesses, then the Bellocian method is dangerously right: right, because without such a method history remains incomplete and even superficial; dangerous, because the humanist instrument is a delicate rapier and not one to be used without caution, skill, and human understanding. One cannot affirm that Belloc always kept the necessary balance, but he kept it steadily enough through a lifetime of historical labour to have bequeathed us a kind of history rarely written in these days, or in any day for that matter: history which respects tradition, both political and religious, and history which respects the human person in all the tissue of good and evil from whence proceeds human action.

Although the use of the technique of "converging probabilities" frequently issues into judgments that are humanist, i.e. judgments about men, Belloc used his method in the earlier years to establish historical truths that are only incidentally concerned with human personality. In these impersonal studies about battles, roads, rivers, etc., Belloc pointed up his polemic against the German Idealist school that refused to deal with *things*. *The Stane Street*, written in 1913, is possibly the most brilliant success he achieved in this kind of historical investigation. Although the book was severely written, with little of the high rhetoric associated with much of Belloc's history, there are two passages that reveal Belloc's attack against historical idealism.

Let me not be misunderstood; the repeated view that Britain was a sparsely inhabited and only partially Romanised province, is one which no one today with a care for historical truth will maintain. It arose in that hypothetical and North German school of history which prefers to accumulate facts rather than co-ordinate evidence; which delights to give guesswork an equal rank with record, and invariably to oppose that guesswork against the tradition of civilization . . . there has grown up a deplorable academic habit which will build most readily upon the very absence of proof, and one must refute such falsehood before one can proceed to truth . . . *the mere lack of evidence is used for the purposes of confident negation* . . . it is the peculiar disease of our time in this province of inquiry.

For instance, we know nothing of London between the time when Imperial Rome still taxed and administered Britain and the seventh century, when, with the return of the Catholic Church, writing and record returned. Wherefore a whole school has risen which will solemnly maintain the fantastical theory that London in the interval did—what? why, ceased to exist!

No one who has had the good fortune to escape from the influence of the Universities will be ready to believe that they make themselves responsible for so amazing a statement. It is none the less true. Because we do not know what happened to London between one fixed date . . . and another . . . therefore it has been solemnly put forward under academic authority that London in the interval disappeared!

It is folly, of course. It is as clear an abandonment of common sense as it would be to deny the existence of our homes during the hours when we happen to be absent from them.[44]

It is amusing to note that one phrase in the above passage was repeated almost verbatim twenty years later, when Belloc wrote of his dead companion Chesterton, that "he had the singular good fortune to have escaped the University." He wrote this phrase in a context dealing with Chesterton's *realism*. This was the same Chesterton who had said that the only sin was "to call green grass grey." It was the same Chesterton who saw with his friend that there is one, implicit, rarely articulated first principle behind the modern mind: *things are not what they seem to be;* the postulate of an impoverished universe, as it has been called. Whig history was one enemy; but the great enemy against which Belloc directed his historical guns was German *Historismus,* the child of Hegelian idealism, and the enemy of reality.

The development of historiography and the application of scientific techniques to historical evidence arose in Germany and was saddled from the outset by a philosophy that was utterly contemptuous of realism and of the common sense of mankind that accepts implicitly the proposition that "things are." If historical method had grown up unencumbered by ideological weeds, the Western World would never have seen the great destructive attack made on Scripture in the last half of the nineteenth century by German scholarship. It seems reasonable to assume that the new scholarly techniques would have aided men like Belloc in exploding the older Whig myths. Things did not happen that way, because the academic mind behind the new method was corrupted with the pride of idealism. It was a mind diseased to the core that laid its hands on everything hitherto held sacred and true by the united conscience of Christendom. German historical research, around the last quarter of the nineteenth century, touched nothing that it did not negate: filial traditions, the lore of the old rooted peasantries of Europe, religious symbolism whose meaning had been settled for centuries, finally Scripture itself.

This was one of the Barbarians who can never build, but who can only destroy that from which he feeds. Chesterton fought the same battle against these iconoclasts on the level of comparative religion that Belloc fought on the level of secular history. They united in an assault against the idol-breakers, against that mentality that refuses to look and see what is there to be seen. Their enemy was a mind primed by two hundred years of an idealism that had permeated every artery of thought and action with a suspicion of being, a truculence before the things which are. If the things which engage the senses and call forth the assent of the intellect interfere with academic theory, then the things are thrown away, and the theory wins the day. If physical evidence attests to a late and active Roman influence in ancient Britain, and in so doing contradicts official dogma, then the evidence is to be ignored or explained away. If the physical evidence of a document attests to its authenticity, when a theory insists that it be a fraud, why then the document is a fraud. If reason and the senses attest to an existing world, and philosophy proclaims the contrary, then so much the worse for the world.

Belloc keenly grasped the destructive tendencies at work within the Western intelligentsia, which insisted on fencing itself off from the world by weaving around itself fabric upon fabric of theory. He had nothing but contempt for the scholar who lives in a world of images, unrelated to existing things. The typical Intellectual[45] inevitably commences to think in terms of, let us say, maps coloured this way and that; he judges peoples and ideas according to the standards of textbooks and fashionable opinions; he sees the human person in the light of statistical tables (what Belloc could have done with the American School of Education mentality!); he measures reality by rulers laid on sheets of cut cardboard, and by sums reckoned on pads of paper. This sort of thing, typified and caused by idealism, breeds jingoism, pacifism, internationalism, and other brands of ideologies unrelated to reality, and conformed to nothing but systems of phantasy and imagery.

Belloc's historical attack against German *Historismus* must be coupled with his social satire. Both functioned as part of the same polemic against "the Barbarian." As a social satirist he sprayed his irony like acid on this mythological world that has come upon the West. Dozens of his essays and all of his nonsense novels are aimed at exposing and ridiculing the contemporary loss of the sense for reality. Belloc penetrated, sometimes almost inarticulately, into the core of the business: if man is removed from being he cannot be himself, and if he cannot be himself, he cannot enter into the City of God, without which there is neither happiness here nor beatitude beyond. This realization of his rendered him the great iconoclast of the iconoclasts: he broke the idols of the idol breakers. Science he openly branded "the enemy of the truth." Industrial Capitalism was the "Servile State," and the Successful Business Man was a "share shuffler," a "liar and thief"; art was a "stinking trade," because he knew well enough that this would blood the solemnity of the *avant-garde;* advertising he labels a "disgusting lie." The servants of the rich are consigned to the bottom of hell, and polite society is damned with the incomparable:

> Good morning, Algernon: Good morning, Percy.
> Good morning, Mrs. Roebeck. Christ have mercy![46]

The attack against academic idealism was but the center of Belloc's broader assault, carried out through a dozen different artistic media, against the *Zeitgeist.* To grasp the essence of Belloc's integrated Christian humanism is to possess the key to understanding his position as a satirist and controversialist. This age, Belloc repeats over and over again, is not at one with the destiny worthy of a man.

Belloc is ever hammering home one message: shake off this bad dream, and look once again at reality, at being, at Creation. "Dear reader, read less and sail more."

In one of his farewell essays to Chesterton, Belloc declared that the prime glory of his friend was to have seen things as they are. In his own turn, and in his own way, that was Belloc's chief excellence, as it is the chief excellence of any man who can claim right to public respect or cultural frame.

Belloc, principally through his historical work, fought a battle that was spiritual in origin. On the whole Belloc's attack seems to have been less effective than Chesterton's, because Chesterton brought to the battle an amazing good humour and charity for the enemy. He slaps his foe on the back, jokes with him, and enjoys himself hugely. Belloc *publicly* glowers over against the foe. He was always the Roman soldier holding the citadel against the savage from without. Belloc brought to his task an extremely lucid reason, French not only in its incisive keenness, but in its cynicism as well. He could rarely accept the good will of men who opposed his judgments. They were either fools or liars.

There is some irony in Belloc's judgment that Chesterton's effectiveness was blunted because of his charity. For once, Belloc's realism broke down, as does the realism of the French break down, from time to time, when faced with some great simplicity. It was Chesterton's very "weakness" (in Belloc's eyes) that rendered him the more effective of the two in this one aspect of their work: the polemic against un-realism. Chesterton won by his very simplicity, and by the greatness of his childlike vision—so sane and so just, and so full of good will. Belloc made the enemy mad. He stung them, and they reacted in the most deadly way possible. They ignored him after a time, so that today

Belloc remains a writer who has not been tried and found wanting, but who has simply not been tried at all.

Possibly Belloc was *too* effective in his war against the Dons. He made fools of them, and then he insisted on rubbing it in. There is an essay in *Hills and the Sea* called "The Roman Road." It is like many of Belloc's essays: first there is a bathing from the springs of something *in being*, which is soaked into the author's substance through his senses. Then he brings his intellect to bear on whatever it is that has engaged his whole personality, and some judgment is passed. Frequently, the judgment is moral in character. In this particular essay, Belloc relates the story of a ride he took on his horse "Monster" over the old road which presents "an eternal example" of what Rome could do.

. . . That sign of Roman occupation, the modern word "Cold Harbour," is scattered up and down it. There are Roman pavements on it. It goes plumb straight for miles, and at times, wherever it crosses undisturbed land, it is three or four feet above the level of the down. Here then, was a feast for the learned: since certainly the more obvious a thing is, the more glory there must be in denying it . . . just as they will deny that Austerlitz was fought in spite of Trafalgar, or that the Gospel of Saint John is the Gospel of Saint John.

Here, then, sitting upon this Roman road I considered the nature of such men and when I had thought out carefully where the nearest Don might be at the moment, I decided that he was at least twenty-three miles away, and I was very glad: for it permitted me to contemplate the road with common sense, and with Faith, which is Common Sense transfigured; and I could see the Legionaries climbing the hill . . . But chiefly there returned as I gazed the delicious thought that learned men, laborious and heavily endowed, had denied the *existence* of this Roman road . . . Here was a piece of pedantry and skepticism which might make some men weep and some men stamp with irritation . . . but which fed in my own spirit a fountain of pure joy. As I considered carefully what kind of man it is who denies these things; the kind of way he talks; the kind of face he has; the kind of book he writes; the kind of publisher who chisels him; and the kind of way in which his works are bound . . . With every moment my elation grew greater and more impetuous . . . But as they brought me beer and bacon that evening, and I toasted the morning, the memory of things past, I said to myself: "Oxford, Cambridge, Dublin, Durham—you four great Universities—you terrors of Europe— that road is older than you: and meanwhile I drink to your continued healths, and let us have a little room . . . air, give us air, good people. I stifle when I think of you."[47]

No wonder he was ignored! What else could they do with a man like that? Once he subjected his own master-piece, *The Path to Rome*, to the techniques and presuppo-sitions of the "Higher Criticism," and he proved his own book to have been written probably as early as the year 2006. It was all high and hilarious fun, until the enraged Catholic, the dedicated man, flashed out in the last lines: "That is how the damned fools write: and with brains of that standard Germans ask me to deny my God."[48]

Belloc's whole historical practice cannot be understood if it is viewed simply as a reaction against Whiggery. It is more pointedly a reaction against Historicism. To this negative side of his work must be added an insight, as indicated, into a position that is at once traditional, theo-centric, humanist, and because of the union of these things —*causal*. If this were all Belloc did as an historian, the palm of high accomplishment would have been his. But his superb art added the ring of greatness. Belloc the Grizzle-beard was never abstracted from Belloc the Poet, and from Belloc the Sailor. He always entered into the past as the whole man, the Four Men. After hunting down innumer-able details which gave vividness to the drama of the past. he re-enacted the story by an act of imaginative reconstruc-tion. Belloc personally possessed that English gift of visual imagination that he attributed to Milton. The unification of history and art, played down but never totally suppressed in the general histories and monographs, blazed forth in the biographies so powerfully that time was almost physically conquered. Belloc's biographical work shows a constant shifting between a universal view that sees the whole of Christendom, and an approach that frames the present in a series of vividly sketched vignettes. He could transfigure the past. He would haunt the scenes of great battles and stand in these fields of decision, now emptied of their glory; his appearance would be timed to the month and day, and if the exact weather conditions of history did not prevail, he returned until they did. Some poetic power, the exact nature of which he often pondered and never discovered to his satisfaction, was given him, and the past would roll back before him. A vast and intimate knowledge of the minutiae of history, informed by his sweeping vision, seemed to touch the things and places once sanctified or defiled by men and actions past. Listen to him as the drums of Wattignies roll down the centuries:

The sleepless men had been launched at last, the hollow lanes were full of them swarming upward: the fields were ribbed with their open lines, and as they charged they sang.

Immortal song! The pen has no power over colour or over music, but though I cannot paint their lively fury or make heard their notes of triumph yet I have heard them singing: I have seen their faces as they cleared the last hedges of the rise and struck the 3,000 upon every side.

. . . Two charges disputed their certain victory. First, the Hungarian cavalry . . . then the Royal Bourbon, emigrants, nobles, swept upon the French, heads down, ready to spend themselves largely into death. They streamed with the huge white flag of the old Monarchy above them, the faint silver lilies were upon it, and from either rank the cries that were shouted in defiance were of the same tongue which since Christendom began has so perpetually been heard along all the battle fronts of Christendom . . . These also failed: a symbol in name and in flag and in valour of that great, once good, and very ancient thing which God now disapproved.[49]

This kind of writing is art, literary art at its best, wedded here to historical judgment, keen sensibility, and poetic vision. This felicitous unity of things not often found together is not a rare perfection, blessing a dozen odd pages of a life of historical writing; it is steady, filling volume after volume, informing and pleasing through the years; a life's work of art in which the intended result obtains: the resurrection of the past, so that the men of the West can come into their own once again.

Chapter Three

CHRISTENDOM:
"ESTO PERPETUA"

Today when Western man thinks of Christendom, he thinks of an historical order that is dead, or he thinks of an academic humanist tradition that synthesizes the Greek and Roman heritage with the doctrinal truths of the Faith. Western man rarely thinks of himself as being a man in Christendom, for Christendom is no longer a place, existing in space, enduring in time.

Hilaire Belloc was the last representative of a long tradition of Catholic thinkers who actually thought of the Christian Unity in terms of a cultural and geographical order minted into a unity by the genius of the Faith. His understanding of Christendom is the most serious problem facing anyone who would penetrate his thought. Belloc has been accused of identifying Western Europe and Catholicism to the point where it would appear that the Universal Religion was a uniquely Latin thing that carried with it of necessity the temporal and cultural trappings of Mediterranean regionalism. "Europe is the Faith, and the Faith is Europe."

Belloc's position is neither so obviously naive as his critics would assert, nor can it be identified with the attitude of most contemporary Christians when they think of "Chris-

tendom." In the first place it is simply false to assert that
he identified Catholicism necessarily with Western Europe.
He expressly states the contrary in the famous and controversial *Europe and the Faith*.[50] Operative behind his pas-
sionate and concrete love of European Catholicism is a
doctrinal position that can be stated rather simply: grace
perfects nature, and grace can operate in human nature at
any time and under any conditions, but grace operates the
better, the more perfected is man on the natural level.

It may be taken that whatever form truth takes among men
will be the more perfect in proportion as the men who receive
that form are more fully men. The whole of truth can never
be comprehended by anything finite; and truth as it appears to
this species or to that is most true when the type which receives
it is the healthiest and the most normal of its own kind.[51]

Linked with this doctrinal position is his favorite historical thesis that Roman Europe represented the very best
man had achieved on the temporal level of existence prior
to the advent of the Son of God. In Rome man began to
come into his own; in Rome man discovered the possibility
of an immortal destiny, because Rome had conceived, even
if imperfectly, the nature of human dignity. Roman man
is Myself, the Four Men—integrated on one level of life
but realizing the essential incompletion of his own handi-
work. Christianity came into the Empire and found there
a mentality peculiarly apt for the reception of the Gospel.
It was with such stuff that the Church molded Western
Europe. The result was Christendom.

The conception of Christendom lies at the heart of Belloc's Christian humanism. The necessity for the Faith to
penetrate a culture and erect a civilization that bears her
lineaments is both a deduction from Belloc's humanism and
an historical cause of his humanism, though it is principally
the latter.

Let us first look to the matter theoretically. There is no consciously articulated "philosophy of Christendom" in Belloc, and this for two reasons: Christendom was an historical fact in his eyes; you do not theorize about the possibility of that which *is*; one Thing had preserved the best of the Roman Order, had sanctified the human hearth, and had worked toward the erection of a social and personal dignity unheard-of in late nineteenth- and early twentieth-century England—and this one institution was the Roman Catholic Church; secondly, and this is a weakness in his armour, Belloc had little interest in (or talent for) purely philosophical and theological issues as such; outside of a vigorous defence of the validity of the human reason against skepticism, and an almost inarticulate loathing of German Idealism, he remained aloof from formal philosophy. Christendom is not a "concept" or a "thesis" for him: she is Europe and the ages.

Belloc's failure to elaborate a *philosophical* defence, as well as an historical defence, of the theory of Christendom has left his whole position in jeopardy. Today many highly reputable minds are questioning the validity of the very *idea* of a Christendom. The attack is psychologically understandable. The older European Order, first wounded by the Reformation, then weakened spiritually by four centuries of rationalism, nationalism, and secular liberalism, now physically and morally ruined by the social conflicts produced by industrial capitalism, has been rubbled possibly beyond repair by two world wars. The Christian community will survive in the new era now being born, it is said, only if she shakes herself free from the husks of a culture that no longer exists. Today the East is throwing off its shackles, and if the Faith is to penetrate into the rising self-consciousness of these peoples, it must come as something native to themselves. To cling to an identification of Catholicism and European Catholicism is not only bad theology, it is bad policy. Catholicism is supra-temporal and can never be associated essentially with any of the passing cultural forms that she blesses. It is, then, impossible to speak of a Christen*dom* as being some one unique cultural reality, whose soul is the Faith.

There is more than a little truth to the above reasoning, and there can be no doubt that Belloc's dogged passion for complete, final integration and his deep love for the European Order rendered him temperamentally incapable of realizing the *concrete* possibility of the Faith's taking root in a non-European form. To separate the Faith from the freedom and the institutions of the West was in his eyes to divorce the mother from its child, and to desecrate that historical unity that centuries had hallowed. If he overstated his case, it can be affirmed nonetheless that he had a case to overstate.

The weakness of the anti-Bellocian position lies in its sheer abstractionism. In the abstract there is no question but that the Faith is culturally neutral. But historically it is simply false to say that the Church has always been, and could always be, neutral to any given civilization to which she has come, or will come, preaching salvation. The Church could never have sanctified Carthage with its human sacrifice to Moloch; the Church could never have concreted itself in those border cultures that produced the Mystery Cults and flirted with the pantheisms of the East. Belloc fingered a profound historical truth when he declared that as Revelation incarnates itself the better in a man in proportion to that man's natural perfection, so too Revelation has always embodied itself in any culture in relation to the degree of corporate perfection achieved by that society.

If certain cultures as well as certain men seem better disposed to receive Faith than others, it is still true that Faith comes to them as a pure gift. Catholicism did not have to fix itself within the boundaries of the Greco-Roman world. But the historical fact is that it did so. That Rome was more apt to receive the Gospel than were her neighbours is, to Belloc, one of the clearest truths of Western history. Those who accuse Belloc of theoretically tying the Church to Rome confuse two questions: a theological question and an historical question. Doctrinally, the Faith belongs to no one by right; but if the Faith does come to a man, it will come to him as to one formed by a unique set of cultural exigencies, which will aid or will hinder his reception of the Divine Gift. The Faith belongs to no culture by right. Some cultures could never have received her; other cultures could have, but historically they did not. The fact remains that she came into Rome, transformed the Empire and built a Europe that had been humanized to a high level by the already existing Latin Order.

It may here be objected that to connect so closely the worldly foundations of our civilization with the Catholic or universal religion of it, is to limit the latter and to make of it a merely human thing.

The accusation would be historically valueless in any case, for in history we are not concerned with the claims of the supernatural, but with a sequence of proved events in the natural order. But if we leave the province of history and consider that of theology, the argument is equally baseless. Every manifestation of divine influence among men must have its human circumstance of place and time. The Church might have arisen under Divine Providence in any spot: it did, as a fact, spring up in the high *Greek* tide of the Levant and carries to this day the noble Hellenic garb. It might have risen at any time: it did, as a fact, rise just at the inception of that united Imperial Roman system which we are about to examine. It might have carried for its ornaments and have had for its sacred language the accoutrements and the speech of any one of the other great civilizations, living or dead: of Assyria, of Egypt, of Persia, of China, of the Indies. As a matter of historical fact, the Church was so circumstanced in its origins and development that its external accoutrements and its language were those of the Mediterranean, that is, of Greece and Rome: of the Empire.[52]

Such is the principal meaning of *Europe and the Faith:* as a matter of fact the Church arose within the bosom of the Roman Empire; as a matter of fact she alone saved the imperfectly formed humanism of the classical world; it is a fact that this tradition was absorbed into the larger Thing which was the Faith and which made Europe in her own image. If you would find anywhere on this earth a way of living that breathed the spirit of Christianity, you would find it in Western Europe that largely remained faithful through all the attacks from without, and from all the schisms from within. A free peasantry, the sacredness of marriage, the dignity of man, the steady rejection of every Manichean irresponsibility and of every pantheist negation, the sacramental view of the universe: these are to be found in Catholic Europe and wherever else she has stamped her genius, and they are to be found as corporate doctrines tending to actuality nowhere else on this earth.

The Church "lays her foundations in something other," says Belloc, but "out of that something other came the art and the song of the Middle Ages." And he adds his famous taunt to the Englishmen of his day, "and what art or song have you?"[53]

Such is the basic Bellocian doctrine on the historical relationship between Catholicism and European Christendom. And yet he pushes his position even further in a daring move that links him with those early Christians who saw in Rome the special mark of Divine Providence, preparing a way for the Incarnation. As a man never exists outside of the supernatural order, with the result that even his natural perfection is achieved under the impetus of grace, one can say that God is operating with lavish gratuity wherever a cultural organism is found to have reached a certain high level of human perfection. Humanism is crowned by grace, but in a deeper sense, humanism is caused by grace. "The Church makes men," Belloc puts it tersely in one sentence in *The Path to Rome*.[54] It is small wonder, then, that when viewing that sweep of Empire which is the foundation of the West, when seeing that high pitch of humanism that avoided the Eastern nihilisms, when gazing at that magnificent legal structure, imperfect though it was, that had as its end the defining of human dignity—when seeing all these things, it is no wonder Belloc frequently talked like those Latin Fathers who saw in Rome a Unity raised by God to prepare man for the Incarnation.

Grace not only crowns nature but causes nature to flower into its fullness. All human values, tending of isolation and separate destruction outside Catholic Christianity, are unified within the Body of Christ by the bond of Charity. It is, therefore, reasonable to believe that the Roman Order —classical humanism—was created by God for the sake of the preaching of the Gospel. Compare two passages rather closely: one was composed around A.D. 385 by the Christian poet Prudentius; the other was written in 1906 by Hilaire Belloc in his *Esto Perpetua*.

We live in every clime, as if a paternal city enclosed within its single walls citizens of a single birthplace; we are all one in heart within our paternal hearth. Now, men from afar and over land and sea appear before a single and common court; now, for business and the arts they gather together in the great assembly; now, they contract marriages and one people is formed from the mingling of different blood. This has been achieved by so many triumphant successes of the Roman Empire, believe me, that the way has been prepared for Christ's event, a way which the communal friendship of our peace has built under Roman guidance. For, what place could there be for God in a savage world, in the discordant breasts of men and in those who guard their own rights by different laws, as was formerly the case? But, if the mind, from its lofty throne, bridle impulsive rage and the rebellious organs and bring every passion under the sway of reason, then is built a stable way of life; then with surety does it drink in God and live in submission to the one Lord. Omnipotent One, now is Your hour; penetrate the earth where no discord reigns. Now, O Christ, the world accepts You, this world which peace and Rome together hold within their grasp.[55]

Setting aside details and moving to the heart of the text, we could say that the poet has laid down the proclamation of Christendom: a corporate theocentric humanism. Man's personal and social integration exists in order that God may conquer the soul. Now listen to Belloc's passage as he sails away from the African shores and faces once more the Latin Order:

"In Europe, in the river-valleys," I thought, "I will rest and look back, as upon an adventure, towards journey in this African land . . . I shall be back home. I shall come again to inns and little towns . . . and I shall see nothing that the Latin Order has not made." I thought about all these things as the ship drove on.

Europe filled me as I looked out over the bows, and I saluted her though she could not see me nor I her. I considered how she had made us all, how she was our mother and our author, and how in that authority of hers and of her religion a man was free. On this account, although I had no wine (for I had drunk it long before and thrown the bottle overboard), I drank in my soul to her destiny . . .

We pass. There is nothing in ourselves that remains. But do you remain for ever. What happens in this life of ours, which we had from you, *Salva Fide*, I cannot tell: save that it changes and is not taken away. They say that nations perish and that at last the race itself shall decline; it is better for us of the faith to believe that you are preserved, and that your preservation is the standing grace of this world.

It was in this watch of the early morning that I called out to her *"Esto Perpetua!"* which means in her undying language: "You shall not die." . . .[56]

We pass over the matchless splendour of the prose until another time. Suffice it to say that this man has seen something that calls forth that "piety of speech" reminiscent of the seventeenth century.[57] As Prudentius sees classical Roman Europe as caused by God in order to be a highway, a Roman Road, over which will pass the message of the Gospel, so does Belloc look back on this prophecy, fulfilled through a thousand years full of a Christendom, armed, proud, conscious of its destiny. Aware that nations pass and that cultures are subject to the cruel laws of time, he nonetheless prays that historic Christendom may remain one Thing, "the standing grace of this world."

To a contemporary thinker, even a contemporary Christian thinker, Christendom is something apart from himself —an historic era, good in its day, but its day is now done. He stands outside of the old European Unity, for it exists no longer, except perhaps in "the river-valleys," and in the mountains, as yet unpenetrated by technological secularism. *He* looks to a new synthesis of Christianity with the modern world, and in desiring this thing he tends to condemn those who would look back and who would still hope for the Resurrection of Europe.

But Belloc always saw Christendom as some one historic Reality, thrusting itself into the dimension of present time— a Reality within which he has consciously situated himself. Having become one with the men of old Europe (how he knew and loved the peasantry and the soldiery of the Continent, the silent men of South England, and the company of those that sail) he could only look *back* for corporate salvation. To look to a new synthesis that transcended the essential elements of the Roman Order would be for him to destroy himself. You cannot uproot an unalienated man.

Supporting this hidden marriage with his origins is Belloc's firm opposition to the Hegelian conception of history, in which the old is necessarily overcome by the new, and in which nothing historical remains that is not powdered into ashes by an iron determinism. Those men who say that the old Christendom is dead may be right, but when they ground their opinion in an historical determinism, they demonstrate their inability to understand the *organic* nature of a traditional society, in which the past can be renewed through an ever recurrent act of collective memory.

The old European Christendom that Belloc loved so well may never come back; its rich cultural diversity, its personal individualism and patchwork of small property, its shrines, its liberating chaos—these things can have no place in a world committed to the principle of technological and collectivist barbarism. The European way of life died, not because it had to, but because there were not enough men left with the will to keep it alive.

Belloc had the will, but his prayer, "You shall not die," seems a trifle remote in this fifth decade of the century. It seems more and more probable that the Christian community of the future will resemble Communist cells lost in a world given over to the barbarism of faceless men. The Faith may, at some future date, arise out of the new catacombs and be faced with sanctifying a society that is neither humanist nor humane. Belloc recognized this possibility,[58] always believing the contrary more likely. But should a Christian Order commence to arise out of the atomic ruins of a mechanical and industrial desert, it will work again to the erection of a genuinely human order. And should the men of this new age wish to know that freer and broader vision of their half-forgotten fathers, they could do no better than to turn to the work of this last of the rooted men.

If the old Christendom is dead, then a new Christendom will be built in time. Christendom may be considered an "outmoded concept" by some thinkers who consider the modern world to have been a necessity. These intellectuals fail to see that Christendom is rather a fundamental urge, deep within man, grounded in an ontological need for the complete integration of man's spiritual and temporal destinies.

The issue needs further elucidation. There have been so many attacks in recent years against the Bellocian position on the relationship between Europe and Catholicism, and on his understanding of "Christendom," that a thorough airing of the subject is necessary. In the first place, only an irresponsible writer like Sidney Hook would accuse Belloc of identifying the interests of Catholicism with the *ancien régime*.[59] Belloc gloried in the best traditions of the Revolution, and, with the exception of Bernanos, he seems to be the only historian to have grasped the Christian continuity of the new and the older political traditions of Europe. He was so much the Republican that he was duped by the pretensions of Rousseau. The charges of reaction are not worth the dignity of a formal reply. In the second place, those quite responsible men who oppose the Bellocian slogan of "Europe is the Faith" are guilty, not of irresponsibility, but of a lack of intellectual subtlety. To state that the Faith is supra-temporal and is thereby never to be identified with any given civilization is to enunciate a truism, and to miss the point. It is one thing to say that no cultural order is of the essence of the Faith; it is another thing to say that the Faith is of the essence of some given cultural order. The latter is Belloc's position. When the Faith is of the essence of that culture, then that civilization is part of, or coincident with, Christendom. The historical proof of Belloc's point lies in the brutal truth that when that given social order loses the Faith, it ceases to be itself. Such is the meaning of "Europe is the Faith."

More profoundly and more to the heart of the issue is the objection to conceiving Christendom, if there is or has been or will be such, as a place. Today probably all would agree that Christendom is largely a state of mind; but with Belloc the writer of these pages asserts that Christendom *must become a place,* because man is a material as well as a spiritual creature, existing in space, enduring in time. As his inner perfection necessitates the interpenetration of the natural and the supernatural, so too must this inner personal unity be projected externally in a corporate entity that ideally could be bounded geographically, politically, and socially. That God be found in a shrine is a paradox inherent in the very mystery of the Incarnation. That man, once he is Christian, will try to build a house of such a nature that he can say to himself and to his friends, "This is a place in which Christian men will be at home," is the inner meaning of Christendom in the thought of Hilaire Belloc. He always sought out old inns, and it was because he hoped to find lingering there something of the essence of what was once the Christian Inn of Mankind.

In one sense, a Christian is always an exile. In another sense, he is an island; and it is in *this* that is to be found the heart of the need for Christendom—a *corporate* theo-centric humanism—a *place* so penetrated by the Faith that a man who was there could say that "Jesus Christ was in the morning skies."[60]

Belloc grasps the older European Christendom, in its ideals and in the best of its actualities, as a truly human society, permeated from top to bottom with grace, and given direction and destiny by the Universal Faith. Personal perfection necessitates the communal act in which society is built as a home for man. The City of Man exists for the furthering of human perfection. The City must be personal: from this follows Belloc's detestation of impersonal governments. The best government would be one personally exercised by all men, acting together for the common good. Where this democratic society is impossible of fulfillment, the community is best incarnated in a monarchy: one man sums up in himself a people, and one man is responsible to all.

The Bellocian concepts of both democracy and monarchy are not co-extensive with the more usually accepted meanings of those terms. For Belloc democracy is less a static thing than something dynamic. The French erupting into the Revolution, organizing great armies and local governments almost overnight—such is democracy as Belloc sees it. It is the older ideal of the Citizen assuming personal responsibility; it is Drouet accepting history at the crossroads, the Parisians before the Tuileries, man at the barricades. In Belloc's eyes the only surviving democracies in the West are the Swiss cantons and the mountain state of Andorra. Belloc's monarchy is one man, symbolizing a people and its traditions, exercising personal authority, responsible before the law, a public sacrifice to the land. He finds his best example in modern times in the United States of America: in the Office of the Presidency.[61]

A personalist society, be it democratic or monarchical,

will foster those occupations attached directly to fundamentally human needs. Man needs to build; he needs to plant and to plow, to make things with his hands, to incarnate his aspirations in song and the plastic arts; he needs to fight, and he needs to pray. The peasant, the artisan, the soldier, the scholar, the poet, the priest—these will dominate any humanist culture in Belloc's sense of the term. A broad base of well-distributed property will lie under the whole economic organism, insuring the personal character of the *res publica*, stamping it with the mark of humanity. Belloc has little use for a merchant society (exemplified in his eyes by Carthage and Whig England). The merchant necessarily is engaged in furthering his own profit, and he must prosper by feeding on those elements within the community that are productive. Merchants will always be in a society, but if the state is controlled by their spirit, then the City of Man is finished. Profit, not human perfection, is the bourgeois ideal. Viewed ideally, Belloc's humanist society, on which he constructed his distributist economics, would be characterized by a rich multiplicity of functions rooted in fundamental human drives.

The City of Man is the extension, the natural fulfillment, and the guarantee of the personal integration symbolized by *The Four Men*. Man, unalienated in the densities of his own subjectivity, achieves an objective corporate unity with his fellows. Even the most penetrating and private of natural mysteries, that of poetic creation, finds its full significance only in the Forum. "For the Poet, though divine, is a servant. He is the god of the house of Admetus; and not all his fellowship with heaven would make him what he is did he not bring to birth the struggling song, as yet undelivered in his fellow men."[62]

Belloc's ideal of the good social order is not a utopia. The "proprietary state," as he calls it, is the natural order of things for men, and only the parochialism of a vision that cannot see beyond the last century on the Continent, or beyond the Reformation in England, would insist on viewing industrial capitalism and the consequent Communist or Collectivist dreariness as advances beyond the simple humanist order that meshes so beautifully with human nature. In his final books, written just before the catastrophe of World War II, Belloc declared that Denmark and Ireland, and the Portugal of Salazar, were the most decent states within which man could find his personal and social perfection. In contemporary cultural theory, there are a number of parallels to Belloc's distributist or proprietary ideal. In the United States a similar conception can be found in the thought of the Southern Critics. In England, Mr. T. S. Eliot has advanced a like doctrine in his *Notes Toward a Definition of Culture*. Both men conceive of culture as fundamentally traditional, i.e. organic. Both see culture as dual: in one dimension it is familial and private; the attachment of the individual to his ancestral home and to the proven ways of doing things assures a rhythmic continuity to society that expresses itself in local patriotism and the love for the place which is one's own; status rather than contract is the ideal, for in status is to be found peace, both personal and public; on another dimension culture is public, and the plurality of economic life is given a unity which flowers in political, artistic, and religious life. However, two radical divergencies in the thought of Eliot and Belloc decisively separate their respective humanisms. Eliot's society is aristocratic and post-Reformation English in inspiration; Belloc's is either democratic or monarchical, and therefore egalitarian, which is to say that it is Latin and Catholic in spirit. Eliot sees religious conflicts as making for a richer cultural diversity. For Belloc the Reformation and the rending of Christendom is the greatest scandal in the story of the West.

In spite of the French antecedents of Belloc's social ideals, his proprietary traditions are rooted deeply in the English past. Most anti-collectivist thinking in the English-speaking world today looks to Burke and the theory of prescriptive politics. But for all his conservatism, Burke never succeeded in dispelling the Whig curse. There is another tradition that runs back, like a narrow and straight road, through Chesterton and Belloc to the Tory-Radicalism of William Cobbett, and beyond to the Cavaliers and to the King who died for England; there the road broadens into a great highway filled with the yeomen who rose in the Pilgrimage of Grace. And beyond all this stands the high medieval vision of Fortesque: a vision of a land of free men, eating and drinking their own, owing allegiance neither to aristocrat nor capitalist, but to God and England alone.

Such is the City of Man in Hilaire Belloc's thought. But this City, Belloc indicates time and again, *is not of itself.* It has no fully independent existence of its own, nor can it ever be a completely autonomous reality. For it to be at all, it must flourish within the higher City which is the City of God. Just as the individual man can find his natural perfection only by losing himself in Christ, so too can the community of all men find its soul only within the bosom of Christian Wisdom. Religious truth, absolute and unquestioned, not only guarantees but causes a God-oriented humanist culture to come into its own. The sacredness of the person and the eternal relationship he bears to God through Christ are truths of an order which is not human, but these truths act within the bowels of society as Divine Seeds, conceiving in time a temporal order both personal and free. This order is Christendom. It is not the City of God, but it is within that City, and it is what it is because it is the child of Faith.

There is a City full, as are all Cities, of halt and maim, blind and evil and the rest: but it is the City of God . . . There are not two such cities on earth. There is One.

Within that household the human spirit has roof and hearth. Outside it, is the night.[63]

Conclusion

THE FUTURE PLACE OF HILAIRE BELLOC IN ENGLISH LETTERS

HE WAS the finest prose stylist of his generation. His art was a habit, possessed at the center of his being by a man who was conscious of his own power. John Edward Dineen has noted how writers of such diverse interests and talents as Rupert Brooke, Ford Madox Ford and Max Beerbohm have paid homage to the literary genius of Hilaire Belloc.[64] Baring's famous tribute is well known: "grave prose like the mellow tones of a beautifully played 'cello . . . solemn, melancholy and majestic." Belloc's prose at its finest was what great prose ought to be: a sensitive instrument adapted to express, with great precision and subtle nuance, the complex genius of its creator. His was an artistry that was largely unmannered, simple, sparing in metaphor, and still remarkably rich: a prose in a line that stretches back to the origins of classical English. "No man," says Lord Tweedsmuir, "has attained more perfectly to the 'piety of speech' of the seventeenth century; no man has written purer and nobler prose in the great tradition."[65]

It is no exaggeration to say that Belloc's prose, rooted as it was in the highest literary tradition, will be read as long as English prose is read by men trained in that great heritage. Belloc often put forth the older ideal that prose should minister rigidly to meaning. To this end he developed an unadorned, plain style as the apt instrument for the elucidation of his political and sociological ideas. *The Restoration of Property*, *The House of Commons and Monarchy*, *The Stane Street* and, most especially, *The Servile State* are the finest examples of Belloc's working in a manner that is almost dry in its cold lucidity. The writing in these books is severely unrhetorical and refreshingly free from the unavoidable pedantries of contemporary academic prose; here Belloc achieves personality in his style only by the constant vigour that informs the whole with an almost military character: *this* Belloc is the French logician who can make an idea march to a conclusion. Belloc's plain style recalls the older Oxford manner and suggests the Newman of the *Parochial Sermons* and *The Arians of the Fourth Century*. Belloc's lyricism is found perhaps at the height of its perfection in *The Path to Rome*, *Esto Perpetua*, and in the little-known translation of Bedier's *The Romance of Tristan and Iseult*. But for vintage Belloc, we must turn to the essays, and most especially to *Hills and the Sea*. There is the grave style of "The Death of a Ship"; there is the delicious parody of his grave style in "The Lost Manuscript." Then there is the anecdotal Belloc telling a story for the sheer love of adventure recalled. There is the humorous Belloc of the Great Fool passages. Finally there is the summing up of a life's vision—once again, *Esto Perpetua*.

In the light of such an incomparable artistic mastery, why is it that Belloc's reputation has suffered so severely within the last fifteen years? Part of the neglect is probably due to the fate of his own generation. The whole Edwardian and Georgian period is engulfed under the snobbery of the *avant-garde*. The heartiness, the zest for existence, the enormous Elizabethan interest in almost everything, the sheer magnificence of the Edwardians seem pretentious and a trifle adolescent to a youth who has aged young in an old world now dead. The Bellocs and Barings and Shaws, diving into the ocean fully clad in evening dress, seem somewhat beside the point to a generation embittered in the fires of World War II. The Belloc who carried burgundy through the streets of Rye tires the grim and somewhat desperate intellectual of the day.

A change in fashion partially accounts for Belloc's decline in popularity, but there is something deeper than mere fashion. If Belloc is not understood today, it may be because his own brand of Christian integration has become almost impossible of achievement at this late date in the disintegration of the Western World. Most of us are not rooted men; we do not live in a traditional culture, and to pretend to do so would be to fall into an archaic lie. The Christian living in the center of an industrialized secularism has no Grizzlebeard. His Sailor is dead and his Poet is without sustenance. Belloc's "corporate memories," and Mr. Eliot's "piety for the dead," can be, at best, only truncated actualities and ideals impossible of immediate achievement. This is the age of *Unheimlichkeit*. Man is no longer at home.

Thinking men turn to those artists who can read the hidden depths of the contemporary soul, and who can reveal the nature of the homelessness of modern man. Thinking Christians turn to the vision of a Mauriac or of a Greene; they look to an aesthetic penetration into the human soul as it actually passes by on the anonymous pavements of the modern world. These men are listened to because they have captured the wounded spirit of the day.

Truth, particularly artistic truth, is not pragmatic. But artistic popularity always is. He who can speak to a man will be heard. Belloc cannot speak to the latter-day man.

Belloc can only echo the suppressed conscience of those millions of silent men—the men who bend over nets and who rest on their plows and who say nothing—the men who still bear within themselves the dreams and passions of Christendom: the love of one's own, the feel for the soil, the sense of arms, the hunger for certitude. Belloc speaks for the underground of Europe.

But in some future time, possibly not remote, when New Man will have exhausted himself attempting to escape his destiny, when he will have tried all the doors leading nowhere, when he will have sickened of paper humanisms, he may turn to the gnarled wisdom and the eternal youth of this last guardian of the West. If he does, he will learn what it means to be a man.

NOTES

(1) G. K. Chesterton, *The Autobiography of G. K. Chesterton* (Sheed & Ward, New York, 1936), pp. 222–8.

(2) *The Four Men*, p. 3.

(3) *Ibid.*, p. 300.

(4) *Ibid.*, pp. 302–3.

(5) *Ibid.*, p. 303.

(6) *Ibid.*, pp. 304–5.

(7) Raymond Las Vergnas, *Chesterton, Belloc, and Baring* (Sheed & Ward, New York, 1938), pp. 79–80.

(8) On at least three different occasions, in the midst of passages that relate intense spiritual crisis, Belloc reverts to the "Myself" device. These passages will be discussed later on in the chapter.

(9) *The Four Men*, p. 56.

(10) T. S. Eliot, *Notes Towards the Definition of Culture* (Harcourt, Brace & Co., New York), p. 42.

(11) Belloc's "Poet," as indicated, is in the Platonic conception of poetry: poetry as the intimation of the "divine." What a contemporary critic would consider essential to a poet, keen sensibility, is found in Belloc's "Sailor."

(12) "The Autumn and the Fall of Leaves," *Hills and the Sea*, pp. 300–1.

(13) *Path to Rome*, p. 118.

(14) "The Autumn and the Fall of Leaves," *Hills and the Sea*, p. 311.

(15) *Ibid.*, p. 311.

(16) Hugh Kenner, *Paradox in Chesterton* (Sheed & Ward, New York, 1947), *passim*.

(17) *Elizabethan Commentary*, p. 170.

(18) *Towns of Destiny*, p. 235.

(19) *Ibid.*, p. 238.

(20) "A Remaining Christmas," *A Conversation With a Cat*, p. 296.

(21) "The Opportunity," *Short*

Talks With the Dead, p. 59.

(22) *Why I Am and Why I Am Not a Catholic*, pp. 10–11.

(23) "Gilbert Keith Chesterton," *The Saturday Review of Literature*, July 4, 1936, p. 4.

(24) Quoted in: Maisie Ward, *Gilbert Keith Chesterton* (Sheed & Ward, New York, 1943), p. 474.

(25) P. D. Murphy, "Hilaire Belloc," *America*, September 25, 1920, pp. 539–40.

(26) *The Path to Rome*, p. 161.

(27) *Ibid.*, p. 118.

(28) "The Idea of a Pilgrimage," *Hills and the Sea*, p. 266.

(29) *Esto Perpetua*, pp. 188–9.

(30) "Arles," *Hills and the Sea*, p. 87.

(31) *The Old Road*, p. 11.

(32) "A Remaining Christmas," *A Conversation With a Cat*, pp. 296–7.

(33) W. H. Auden, *The Enchafed Flood* (Random House, New York, 1951), pp. 3–42.

(34) "The Barbarians," *This and That and the Other*, p. 226.

(35) *Ibid.*, pp. 226–7.

(36) *Esto Perpetua*, p. 177.

(37) *The Old Road*, p. 9.

(38) "A Remaining Christmas," *A Conversation With a Cat*, pp. 296–7.

(39) *Mr. Belloc Still Objects*, p. 42.

(40) Douglas Jerrold, "Hilaire Belloc and the Counter Reformation," *For Hilaire Belloc*, ed. by Douglas Woodruff (Sheed & Ward, New York, 1942), pp. 1–10.

(41) *Europe and the Faith*, pp. viii-ix.

(42) *This and That and the Other*, p. 220.

(43) *Charles I, King of England*, pp. 72–3.

(44) *The Stane Street*, pp. 144–5.

(45) Cf. Belloc's analysis in "Reality," *First and Last*, pp. 69–74.

(46) "On Mundane Acquaintances," *Sonnets and Verse* (Sheed & Ward, New York, 1944), p. 168.

(47) "The Roman Road," *Hills and the Sea*, pp. 222–3.

(48) "The Higher Criticism," *This and That and the Other*, p. 247.

(49) *Marie Antoinette*, pp. 553–4.

(50) Cf. note 52.

(51) "The Men of the Desert," *Hills and the Sea*, p. 249.

(52) *Europe and the Faith*, pp. 4–5.

(53) *The Path to Rome*, p. 351.

(54) *Loc. cit.*

(55) Prudentius, *Contra Symmachum*, PM, 2.609–635.

(56) *Esto Perpetua*, pp. 188–9.

(57) The phrase is Lord Tweedsmuir's; *Pilgrim's Way*, pp. 48–9.

(58) *Survivals and New Arrivals*, p. 219.

(59) Sidney Hook, *The Hero in History* (The Humanities Press, New York, 1943), pp. 119, 123. (There is hidden irony, and humour as well, in Hook's judgment. He discusses a short essay written by Belloc that appeared in a volume called "If, Or History Rewritten"; Belloc speculated, in his essay, on what France would have been like had the Revolution failed through the Royal Family's escaping from the country. Hook, aware of Belloc's fame as a Catholic apologist, simply assumes Belloc to imagine a modern Europe continuing the best traditions of Christendom, had the Revolution failed. But the contrary is the case. Belloc guesses—rightly or wrongly is beside the point here—that the Faith would practically be dead on the Continent had the Revolution failed. It is difficult to see how Hook could have read the piece and said what he did.)

(60) *Sonnets and Verse*, p. 29.

(61) *The Contrast*, pp. 83–136.

(62) "Talking of Byron," *Short Talks With the Dead*, p. 33.

(63) *Essays of a Catholic Layman in England*, pp. 157, 305.

(64) John Edward Dineen, introduction to *Selected Essays by Hilaire Belloc*, compiled by J. E. Dineen (J. B. Lippincott Co., Philadelphia, 1936), p. 6.

(65) Lord Tweedsmuir, *Pilgrim's Way, An Essay in Recollection*, pp. 48–9.

LIST OF EDITIONS CITED

The Four Men (Thomas Nelson & Sons, London, 1906).
Hills and the Sea (Charles Scribner's Sons, New York, 1906).
The Path to Rome (G. P. Putnam's Sons, New York and London, 1902).
Elizabethan Commentary (Cassell & Co., London, 1942).
Towns of Destiny (Robert M. McBride & Co., New York, 1931).
A Conversation With a Cat (Harper & Brothers, New York, 1929).
Short Talks With the Dead and Others (The Cayme Press, Kensington, 1926).
Esto Perpetua (Duckworth, London, 2nd. imp., 1925).
The Old Road (Constable & Co., London, 1911).
This and That and the Other (Methuen & Co., London, 1927).
Europe and the Faith (The Paulist Press, New York, 1920).
Charles I, King of England (J. B. Lippincott Co., London, 1933).
The Stane Street (Constable & Co., London, 1913).
First and Last (Methuen & Co., London, 1924).
Sonnets and Verse (Sheed & Ward, New York, 1944).
Marie Antoinette (G. P. Putnam's Sons, New York and London, 1931).
Survivals and New Arrivals (Macmillan, New York, 1929).
The Contrast (Robert M. McBride & Co., New York, 1924).
Essays of a Catholic Layman in England (Macmillan, New York, 1931).
Mr. Belloc Still Objects (Ecclesiastical Supply Association, Publ. and Imports, San Francisco, 1927).